Johnson's®

Your Baby WITHDRAWN
from birth to 6 months

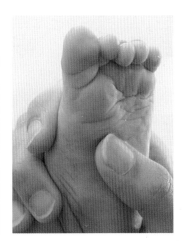

7/03

London, New York, Munich, Melbourne, Delhi

Text by
Katy Holland
For Patrick and Stanley

Project editor Jane Laing
Project art editors Christine Lacey, Glenda Fisher
Senior editor Julia North
Managing art editor Tracey Ward
US senior editor Jill Hamilton
US editor Jane Perlmutter
Production controller Louise Daly
Photography Ruth Jenkinson
Art direction Sally Smallwood

First American Edition, 2002
2 4 6 8 10 9 7 5 3 1

Published in the United States by DK Publishing, Inc.,
95 Madison Avenue, New York, NY 10016

A Cataloging-in-Publication record for this book is
available from the Library of Congress
ISBN 0-7894-8446-3

Reproduced by Colourscan Overseas Pte Ltd, Singapore
Printed by Graphicom, Italy

See our complete catalog at
www.dk.com

Contents

A message to parents from Johnson & Johnson

For more than 100 years, Johnson & Johnson has been caring for babies. Our baby products help mothers and fathers soothe, comfort, and nurture a deep, loving bond with their child through everyday care.

Building on our commitment to children and families, Johnson & Johnson established the Johnson & Johnson Pediatric Institute, LLC. This unique organization promotes continued learning and research in pediatrics, infant development, and pregnancy, building programs and initiatives for professionals, parents, and caregivers that shape the future of children's health worldwide.

Through science, we continue to learn more about our youngest and their physical, cognitive, and emotional development. Parents and caregivers want advice on how to use this learning in their daily lives to complement their basic instincts to love, hold, and talk to their babies.

Good parenting is not a one-size-fits-all formula. With JOHNSON'S® *Child Development* series, we hope to support today's families with the knowledge, guidance, and understanding to help them bring forth the miracle embodied in each and every child.

and sound as one who weighs a strapping 8lb 13oz (4kg). There are no hard rules about weight, although a baby under 5lb 7oz (2.5kg) may cause concern, because it may indicate a lack of nourishment in the womb, or some other complication of pregnancy.

Your baby will be weighed just a few minutes after birth. Many factors will affect this reading, including your own health and birth weight, your diet during pregnancy, placental function, genetics (larger parents usually have larger babies), gender, and race.

Your baby will probably lose weight in the first week after the birth – a drop of around five to eight percent of her birth weight is perfectly normal. Her body has made a sudden adjustment from a dark, peaceful, watery environment to a bright and noisy world where she breathes air and has to feed through her mouth rather than get nourishment automatically.

By around one to two weeks, your baby will probably have reached her birth weight again.

The Apgar score

As soon as your baby is born, a delivery nurse or pediatrician will evaluate her to check her well-being. This Apgar evaluation – named after its creator, Virginia Apgar – is done one minute and five minutes after delivery and helps medical staff ascertain whether your baby needs any immediate extra assistance to adapt to her new environment. The following things are measured:

★ heart rate
★ breathing
★ muscle tone
★ reflex response
★ color.

This score is only an indicator of your baby's general health at birth. It cannot predict how healthy she will be as she grows up or what sort of personality she will have.

Understanding the Apgar score

Each category is given a score of 0, 1, or 2. A score of 2 indicates a good response in the particular area measured. For example, a heart rate over 100 beats per minute would provide a score of 2, as would good respiration, lots of activity, a lusty cry, and a pink color.

These scores are then totaled to give the overall Apgar evaluation (a possible maximum of 10 points).

The vast majority of babies have an Apgar score of 7 or more; only rarely does a baby score a perfect 10. If your baby's Apgar scores are very low in most of the areas measured (for example, if her respiration is irregular, her heart rate is low, and she is pale or limp), she may be given oxygen. If her scores remain low after assistance, she will be taken to a special neonatal care unit for more intensive medical attention.

Your newborn

Many things about your newborn may be surprising to you. For example, most babies are born looking blotchy, wrinkly, and a little "blue" – this is all very normal and their appearance begins to change in just a few days as they grow and develop. Chances are that you and your partner will be completely in awe of your new baby and experiencing many new emotions.

Your baby's head

Unless he was delivered by cesarean section, your baby's head is unlikely to be perfectly round. His skull is made up of soft bones that are designed to give under pressure in order to ease his passage through the birth canal. This

malleability can make his head look slightly misshapen or pointy immediately after birth, especially if he was delivered by vacuum extraction or forceps. This will not have damaged him in any way, and, as he develops, his head will soon return to a more regular shape.

The soft patches on your baby's skull are the fontanels. You may be able to see his pulse beating in this area. If he was born very quickly, he may have tiny blood vessels visible on his face, and his head may look slightly purple, due to the pressure put on it.

Your baby's face

Your baby's face may have a slightly "squashed" appearance, and his eyes may be swollen or puffy from pressure during birth. Don't be surprised if he looks crumpled – he's been putting up with some pretty cramped conditions for a while. Over the next few weeks, he will lose this newborn "scrunched-up" look as his face grows into its new space.

Your baby's skin

At birth, your baby may be covered in a creamy, greasy substance called vernix. This acted as a protective barrier for his skin, preventing it from becoming waterlogged

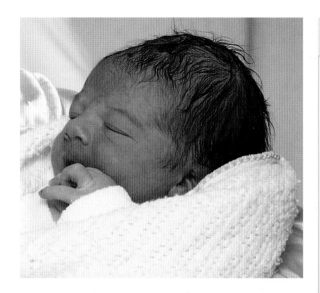

by amniotic fluid in the womb, but it is usually wiped off soon after birth.

His skin may be a little blue at first. It will gradually turn pink as his breathing becomes more regular and circulation improves. If his skin looks "loose" or wrinkly, it's because it hasn't had a chance to build up layers of fat. These will fill out gradually over the next few weeks.

In the first two or three weeks, newborn skin is often dry or flaky, and little white spots known as "milk spots," or milia, are quite common, too: these are enlarged, oily glands and will disappear by themselves.

Your baby's hair

When he was in your womb, your baby was covered with a fine layer of downy hair called lanugo. Some babies, especially those born prematurely, still have some of this hair when they are born. This is completely normal and rubs off during the first few weeks.

Any amount of hair on your baby's head, from none to thick and curly, is normal. Whatever its color or texture now, it will gradually fall out during his first year or so and will be replaced by new hair, which may look quite different.

What can he do?

Your newborn baby is born with an incredible number of skills, all of which equip him to survive in his new environment. Although he has limited voluntary control over his own body or movements, his powers of perception are sharp, and he is primed to take in all the information he needs.

★ **He can communicate by crying and by his behavior.** This is his only way of telling you how he's feeling. He will cry to let you know he is hungry, uncomfortable, or lonely. You will soon learn to recognize and respond to his different cries.

★ **He can see.** Your baby will probably open his eyes almost immediately after birth, even if they don't remain open for long. Although his long-distance vision is blurred at this stage, he will be able to focus on objects that are around 8–10in (20–25cm) away from him, and will be particularly attracted to those objects that have lots of contrast of light and shade (such as your face) and objects that move.

★ **He can hear.** Your baby will also be alert to sounds – especially the sound of your voice, which until now has been muffled by amniotic fluid. Even at this stage, he will be sensitive to the inflections and rhythms of language. Of course, most interesting of all will be a very new sound – that of his own voice.

★ **He can smell.** Your baby's sense of smell is extremely well developed by the time of birth. Once he has learned your particular scent, he will use it to locate you by turning his head in your direction.

Other newborn characteristics

Other "surprises" at birth may include the size of your baby's genitals, which can look swollen because of the hormones that you've passed on to him via the placenta before birth. The swelling should subside within a few days. His cord stump, where the umbilical cord was cut, may also look strange to you. This quickly turns black, and will dry out and fall off in his first few weeks.

First health checkup

Now you have met your new baby, you will want to be reassured that she is in tip-top condition. Within the first hours after birth, a healthcare professional will give her a thorough examination.

The healthcare professional will start by asking you about your baby's eating and sleeping patterns, how often you need to change her diaper, and what her behavior is like. He will also ask how you are feeling and whether you have any concerns about your baby's health. Your baby will then be weighed and measured and the following tests carried out.

● Your baby's heart and lungs will be listened to with a stethoscope.

● The roof of her mouth will be checked to make sure there is no cleft in her palate.

● Her eyes will be examined.

● Her tummy will be felt to check that internal organs, such as liver and kidneys, are the right size and in the right place. The pulses in the groin will also be checked.

● Her genitals will be examined to make sure they are normal. If your baby is a boy, the doctor will check to see whether his testes have descended.

● Her spine will be examined. The doctor will turn her on her tummy to do this, and at the same time he will check that her back passage (anus) is open.

● Her limbs will be checked to make sure they match in length and that her feet are properly aligned, with no sign of club foot (clavicles intact).

● Her hip joints will be examined to make sure they are not dislocated.

Checking your baby's reflexes

The healthcare professional will also test some of your baby's reflex responses. These will give a sound indication that she is generally in good shape, and that her central nervous system is functioning well.

Reflexes are instinctive responses, which help your baby to survive the first few weeks outside the womb. They will disappear when her physical and mental skills have developed and she is able to make more voluntary, conscious movements. There are more than 70 newborn reflexes, but only a selection will be tested. If your baby

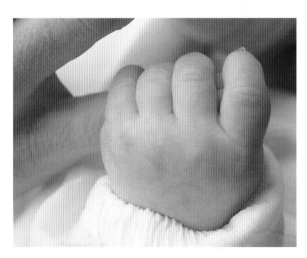

GRASPING REFLEX
The fingers of this baby's hand curl tightly around the finger of the healthcare professional as soon as it touches the baby's palm. Her grasping reflex is still very much intact.

was premature, she won't respond in the same way as a full-term baby, and this will be taken into account.

The grasping reflex

The pediatrician will check your baby's grasp reflex by placing his fingers in the palms of her hands to see if she automatically clings on to them. For many babies, this reflex is so powerful that they can be lifted up by their fingers (although you should never try this). You may also notice your baby's toes curling when you stroke the soles of her feet, as if to grip on to something.

The grasping reflex is generally lost when your baby is around five months old, although the toe-curling may remain for up to a year.

Sucking, rooting, and gagging

Your baby's most basic reflexes include sucking, which ensures that she is able to feed. You may find that she sucks on her own fingers, or on yours, and that she turns automatically toward a nipple or teat if it is brushed against her cheek. This is known as the rooting reflex. Swallowing and gagging – which clear your baby's airways when necessary – are also reflexive.

The Moro reflex

This is also known as the "startle" reflex. Your baby will be undressed and the healthcare professional will hold her, supporting the back of her head with his hand. He will then let her head suddenly drop back a little, which should cause her to throw out her arms and legs with her fingers extended, as though she's trying to find something to cling on to. Your baby will then slowly draw her arms into her body with her fingers clenched and knees bent up to her abdomen. Both sides of your baby's body should respond simultaneously and equally. The Moro reflex disappears at around the age of two months.

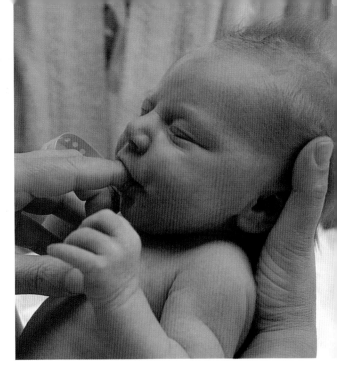

SUCKING REFLEX
This baby shows she will have no trouble sucking from her mother's breast or a teat – she sucks automatically on the finger of the healthcare professional as soon as it is presented to her.

The walking reflex

The healthcare professional may hold your baby under her shoulders so that she is in an upright position with her feet touching a firm surface, to see if she moves her legs in a "walking" action. This reflex disappears at around one month, and has nothing to do with learning to walk; the skill of standing and walking can only be accomplished when her muscles and joints, along with her sense of balance, is much more mature – usually at around 12 months.

The crawling reflex

When your baby is on her tummy, she will automatically assume what appears to be a crawling position, with her bottom high and her knees pulled up under her abdomen. When she kicks her legs, she will be able to shuffle in a vague crawling manner. This behavior will disappear when she is able to lie flat, without curling her legs (usually at around two months).

Premature babies & twins

About 11.5 percent of babies born in the US are premature, or born before 37 weeks' gestation. If your baby is one of them, he will not be ready to cope easily outside the womb, so he will be taken to a special care unit where he will get the help he needs.

How your baby is affected

The earlier he arrives, the smaller your baby will be. If he was very premature, his skin may look almost transparent because it is so thin, and this means he will feel cold in normal room temperatures. For this reason, he will be placed immediately in an incubator, where the temperature can be adjusted to keep him warm. Your baby's cry may be very soft, and he may have difficulty breathing. This is because his respiratory system is still immature. If he is more than two months early, these

Bonding with your premature baby

Although special care is very important for your baby's survival, this can be a very tough time for you. On top of worrying about his health, you may miss the experience of holding, breast-feeding, and bonding with him right after delivery.

Research shows that the more contact a mother has with her premature baby, the more likely the baby is to thrive, so being there and being able to cuddle him, hold his hand, or soothe him with your voice even for short periods can make all the difference.

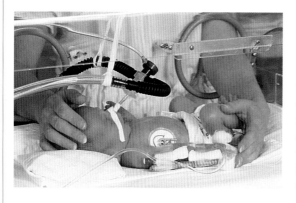

Although it may be difficult, effective bonding can still take place with your baby in an incubator.

★ Ask to see your baby as soon as possible after delivery, and try to be as active as you can in caring for him.

★ Spend as much time with him in the nursery as you can, and even if you cannot hold him, touch him through the holes of the incubator.

★ Breast-feed him if possible, or ask the nurses to help you express milk to feed him; this will stimulate your own milk production so you can nurse him later.

★ Try not to be intimidated by all the machinery.

★ Make sure you understand why your baby needs special treatment. This will help reduce your anxiety.

★ Get as much advice and support as you can. Talk to the nurses who are caring for your baby, your doctor, and midwife. Ask them for information about support networks for parents of premature babies.

THE POWER OF TOUCH
This mother begins to bond with her premature baby by touching his head and legs through the specially designed armholes in the side of the incubator.

breathing difficulties can affect the other organs in his body, which may not get enough oxygen. To ensure this doesn't happen, he will be given extra oxygen, or special equipment may be used temporarily to help him breathe.

The impact on his development

A premature baby's development may be slow and erratic to begin with, but it shouldn't be compared with babies who are born at term. When thinking about his development, first correct his age by calculating how old he would be if he had been born at full term. For example, if he was born two months early, he is unlikely to reach the milestones of a "normal" three-month old baby until he is three months old plus up to two months. At his developmental checks, the healthcare professional will take his "corrected" age into account. And by the time he is about nine months to a year old, he will have "caught up" with babies born at full term.

Twins and multiples

Because of advances in fertility treatments, twin and multiple births are increasing. In the US about one in 75 pregnancies are twins and one in 5,500 are triplets. They are frequently born early and therefore tend to be smaller and lighter than the average newborn, so they often need special care in the first few weeks of life.

Development of twins

Sometimes twins do not follow the same development pattern as other single babies of their age. Some twins seem to "share" the workload, with one excelling in motor skills, such as hand control, while the other perfects social or communication abilities.

Interaction with you is the key to their development, but because of the demands they make on your time it can be hard to make sure twin babies get enough stimulation through play and physical contact. As with all babies, try to take them out for a walk regularly: exposure to new people, sounds, and sights is stimulating in itself.

Take any offers of help to take the pressure off. Pick a set time for playing with your babies every day when you will be able to give each of them your full attention. Choose a time when someone else can be there too, so you can give your twins individual attention. Even a five-minute play with each baby will be of great value.

Bonding

Bonding is a very special process: a wonderful experience through which you and your baby learn to love each other. This relationship may begin to form as soon as you set eyes on your baby, or it may take many months to establish, strengthening every time you interact. Bonding is not only mutually rewarding on an emotional level; it is as crucial to your baby's long-term development as food and warmth.

How you bond with your baby

If your labor went well and your baby was handed to you immediately after delivery, she may respond to you right away by looking at you and perhaps suckling at your breast, and you may feel a surge of love. Your baby will feel the closeness of your body, identify your scent, hear the sound of your voice, look into your eyes, and

perhaps get her first taste of your breast milk. All of these things will calm her and help her to feel secure.

Touching

One of the most powerful ways in which you bond with your baby is through physical closeness and skin-to-skin contact, which brings warmth and security to you both, instilling a sense of well-being. This closeness with your baby is also important for her emotional and physical development. Research has shown, for example, that premature babies thrive from the skin contact involved in "kangaroo care," when babies spend time lying against their mother or father's chest, instead of in an incubator.

Set aside some peaceful time when you can hold your baby against your skin, and enjoy the sense of closeness it brings. Bathe her gently in warm water, holding her securely, and afterwards massage her with baby oil.

Talking

Your baby will love you to talk to her. Even a newborn will respond to the sound of your voice, turning her head towards it and expressing her pleasure by wriggling or kicking. It doesn't matter what you say; she'll love the attention, and you'll enjoy watching her responses.

Look at her when you talk to her. Making eye contact is a great way of communicating, and it will really help to strengthen the level of understanding between you, as well as help her social skills.

Bonding takes time

Bonding is a process, and it may take weeks or even months before you begin to form a loving relationship with your baby, especially if you had a difficult labor or your baby needed special care. It's important not to take on any pressure about how you should or should not feel; go at your own pace, and remember that whether the bond is instant or gradual, sooner or later it will happen as you care for your baby.

Getting the right support

Up to 30 percent of new mothers are reported to have some difficulty in bonding with their babies at first. If you feel like this, try to make sure there is someone – your partner, mother, or a close friend – who can support you and who will also interact with your baby, to take the pressure off you.

Having a new baby is exhausting, so try to cut back on activities around the home, and enlist the help of friends and family. And try to get some sleep when your baby

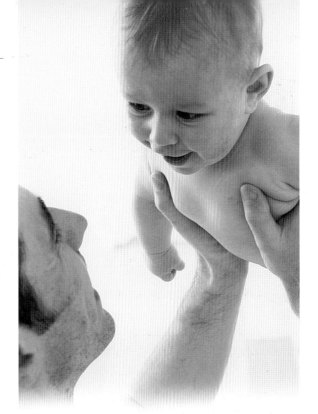

falls asleep during the daytime. Watch out, too, for the postpartum blues. This is the name given to a short period of tearfulness that occurs in many mothers at around three to four days after the birth of the baby. These feelings of being completely unable to cope are due to hormonal changes taking place and usually pass after just a few days.

Postpartum depression

In some cases, mothers who have difficulty bonding are experiencing postpartum depression. Signs of this include lack of energy, irritability, loss of enthusiasm, and feeling overwhelmed and unable to cope for an extended period of time. If you suspect you may be suffering from postpartum depression, talk to your doctor or healthcare professional and ask for support from friends or family. This is absolutely crucial to your recovery.

Spend as much time as possible interacting with your baby. Physical contact stimulates "mothering" hormones, which can have a relaxing effect.

How do dads bond?

Many new fathers have very strong, even passionate, feelings for their offspring, while others may need a little time to adjust. Even though men don't have the same hormones, new fathers are increasingly embracing the role of being an active parent and look forward to "bonding" with the baby with the same enthusiasm as new mothers. Encourage your partner to feel happy in his new role: the more time he can spend with the baby, the stronger his bond will become.

Massaging your baby

Massage is a wonderful way to express your love for your baby – it helps the bonding process between you, calms your baby when he is unsettled, furthers development, and helps to instill a real sense of trust.

The benefits of massage

Loving, positive physical touch will make your baby feel safe and valued, increasing self-esteem and confidence. It has many other physical and emotional benefits, too.

- It will help you communicate with him, to read his body language, and to learn his cues. This can be especially helpful if you and your baby got off to a slow start, perhaps because of early separation.
- It can help relieve pain, promote relaxation, aid digestion, and soothe your baby when he is distressed.

- It can improve circulation and boost his immune system. This is because it helps move lymph fluid around the body, clearing out harmful substances.
- It can tone your baby's muscles and help his joints become more flexible. For this reason it is especially beneficial for premature babies.
- It stimulates growth-promoting hormones. Research shows that babies who are touched a lot grow well – there seems to be a biological connection between stroking and massaging babies and their growth.

When to massage your baby

You can start to massage your baby from around two weeks – you may find it a very helpful way of getting to know him and increasing your confidence in handling him. Choose a time between feedings when he is not sleepy, and do it in a warm room with warm hands.

Getting started

Choose an oil or lotion made specially for babies that can be absorbed into his skin. Keep reapplying the oil to your hands regularly as you massage your baby, to ensure that your movements are soft and smooth.

Undress your baby, putting a towel underneath him to absorb any oil spills or accidents. If you like, just massage one part of his body to begin with. You can then gradually build it up as you gain confidence. In the first few weeks, many babies do not like to be

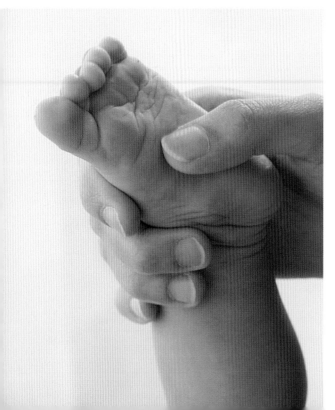

undressed. If this is the case with your baby, do bits of his body at a time so that he is never completely unclothed. For example, leave his undershirt on and concentrate on his legs, perhaps just after you have changed his diaper or when he's had a bath. Then, cover his legs and massage the top part of his body.

Massage technique

Start with your baby lying on his back, and massage the front of his body. Work from the head down, with light strokes, ensuring that both sides of the body are massaged symmetrically. Watch carefully and learn from his reactions. Always stop if he begins to show signs that he is not enjoying it – for example, by turning away from you.

Be very gentle at first, but increase the pressure of the strokes if you feel your baby likes it. Use sweeping movements, and do each part two or three times. When working on small areas, such as his toes, just use your fingertips. On other areas, such as his back, you may find it easier to use two hands.

Head

Lightly massage the crown of his head with circular stokes (avoiding his fontanels), then stroke down the side of his cheeks. Gently massage his forehead, working from the center out, moving over his eyebrows and ears.

Neck, shoulders, and arms

Stroke his neck in downward motions, then move to his shoulders, massaging from the neck outward. You can then slowly move down his arms, gently "wringing" or squeezing them as you go. Then massage his wrists, hands, and fingers, stroking each finger with your fingertips and thumbs.

Chest and tummy

Gently stroke your baby's chest in downward motions, following the curves of his ribs. Rub his tummy in a circular motion, working clockwise and outward from his tummy button with your fingertips.

Legs, feet, and toes

Work from his thighs to his knees, stroking in downward motions around the shins, gently squeezing or "wringing" them as you go. Rub your baby's ankles and feet, stroking from heel to toe, and then concentrate on each toe.

Back

Once you have massaged the front of your baby's body, turn him over and begin massaging his back, again working from the head down.

Your baby's personality

While all young babies have many characteristics and behaviors in common, there are also immense differences between them, even at the very beginning of life. Your baby is an individual who is genetically unique and has already had a particular set of experiences in the womb, during birth, and in the first few months of life. These experiences all play a part in how she settles and responds to the world and to you, and they go a great deal of the way toward defining her character or personality.

The influence of genetics

From the moment of conception, your baby's physical appearance – and many other characteristics – have already been set for life. She inherited half her genes from her mother (via the egg) and half from her father (from the sperm). But because each sperm and egg contains a different combination of genes, she has her own unique appearance, personality, and talents.

Babies vary greatly in the composition of their genes, unless they are identical twins. Many of your baby's physical traits are controlled by these genes, including her hair and eye color, blood group, gender, height, and body shape, for example.

It is also thought that at least some of your baby's character or personality traits are determined by genes – shyness or intelligence, for example, may be inherited. But while genetic make-up can give the potential for your child to be extrovert or shy, academic or sporty, volatile or calm, the way in which she is brought up also has a powerful influence on her personality.

Gender differences

Most experts believe that gender differences, like personality traits, are attributable to a complex mixture of inherited characteristics (nature) and learned behaviors (nurture).

Social expectations have a great bearing on how babies are treated. No matter how "fair" and impartial a parent tries to be, subtle social influences tend to guide behavior. One recent study found that when baby boys were dressed in girls' clothes, they were treated very differently by other parents who had never met the babies before. These baby boys, when dressed in their usual boys' clothes, were treated in a much more physical way than the girl babies and were offered "boys' toys" (noisy toys, cars and trains, for example). When they were dressed as girls, they were treated more delicately and given dolls or teddy bears to cuddle.

Differences in brain development

While outside influences play a major part in the development of your baby, some research suggests that the structure of the brain is responsible for many developmental differences between the sexes. For instance, the right side of the brain, which controls physical activities, is more developed in boys, while the earlier development of the left side of the brain in girls can mean that their fine motor skills and speech develops earlier than in boys.

But, although biological factors may be relevant, they should never be seen as a limitation on your baby's potential. Babies are individuals, and their capacity to learn is far stronger than any biological determinants.

Your baby's temperament

Many factors contribute to forming your baby's character and temperament. Genetics, gender, social environment, number of siblings, all play a large part. Of course, most of these factors are not within your control, and you will be well aware by now that you cannot choose your baby's personality.

But by far the most important of all influences on your baby during the first months – and years – of her life is her relationship with you. You may not be able to choose what "type" of baby you have, but the way you interact with her and respond to her now can have an incredible influence on her developing character.

Whatever personality she has, she will benefit from your love and attention. By following her cues, and being as nurturing as possible, tending to her needs and responding to her cries when she is tiny, you can help her establish a feeling of self-worth that will be invaluable throughout her life. Feeling confident and secure is not only a major asset in life, it is also fundamental to development.

Remember that your baby's personality at this age is constantly evolving. Try not to stick any labels on her, as this can affect the way you respond to her. Nobody can predict what sort of person she will eventually be, but you will undoubtedly delight in discovering all aspects of your baby's emerging personality.

Communication skills

Your baby is born with a strong drive to communicate, and quickly develops many different ways of "talking" to you. He has many different kinds of cry, which he uses to convey different needs. Before he is two months old, he will smile and coo to express pleasure or to engage you in interaction. He is already laying down the foundations of verbal communication.

Crying

Your baby's most effective way of communicating with you in the early months is through crying. He will probably do it a lot because it is the only way he has of letting you know what his needs and feelings are; in a sense, it's his first baby talk. Even your baby's first cry after birth has an important communicative role: it tells the doctor or midwife that his lungs have successfully filled with air for the first time and that he can breathe.

To begin with, you may think that every time your baby cries he makes the same sounds, but you will gradually learn that different noises convey different needs. While every baby's cry is unique, studies have

Body language

When your baby is awake, he is conveying his feelings to his caregivers all the time, in many subtle ways. Eye contact is a very powerful example of this: notice how he catches your eye to engage you in interaction with him, and watches you intently as you talk to him.

Body wriggles and kicks are another powerful means of communicating meaning: he may kick and squirm if he is frustrated or in need of attention, while at other times, these wriggles and jerks are carried out in pleasure and excitement – perhaps at the sound of your voice or to indicate that a particular toy has caught his interest.

He will express dislike or disinterest by turning away from something, point to something he wants (from around six months), and smile as a way of showing pleasure or recognition.

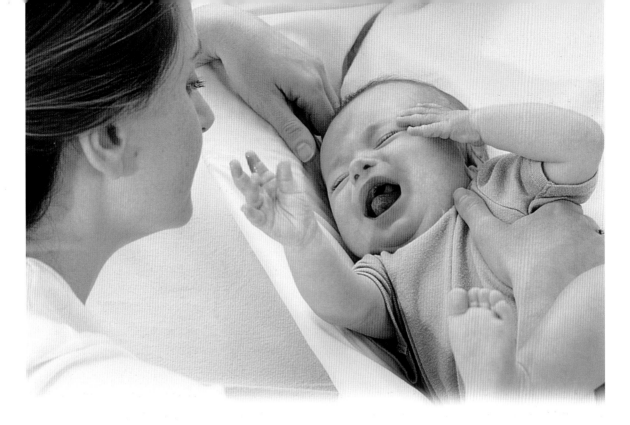

found that the hunger cry often follows a similar pattern of rhythmic noises, and is frequently accompanied by kicking, for example. In contrast, cries of boredom tend to be less regular or coordinated, and may have longer pauses in between as your baby awaits the desired response. Cries of pain are much more intense, and will probably send you running to him.

As you begin to understand the different tones, sounds, and rhythms of your baby's cries, you will be able to attend to his needs quickly and effectively – feeding him when he's hungry and comforting him when he is in pain, for example. This will lessen his need to cry to communicate as time goes on.

What you can do

Quiet babies are often described as well behaved; but a crying baby is not being difficult – he is just letting you know that he is not happy with something. The best thing you can do is respond to him by giving him the attention he needs. Research has shown that, on the whole, babies whose cries are answered quickly tend to be more secure and strongly attached to their parents than those who are left to "cry it out." They also learn at an earlier age to use more varied ways of communication that do not involve crying. By responding to your baby quickly, you are truly letting him know that he has successfully communicated with you, that you are tuned in to his needs, and that he can rely on you. Better still, learn to recognize his body language, so that whenever possible you can intervene before he starts to cry.

Holding him close, talking to him, and giving him lots of attention will give him a sense of security. If you let him know that you are always there when he needs you, he will feel nurtured and cared for.

When crying gets too much

A constantly crying baby can be hard to deal with, but try to remember that your baby is not crying deliberately to frustrate you. Ask friends and relatives to help out, so that you can take some time for yourself to restore your energy levels and give yourself a treat. Take your baby out for a walk and visit a friend. Above all, try not to blame yourself or your baby – it's natural for him to cry, just as it's natural to feel distressed when you cannot seem to do anything to console your baby.

Although it is normal for a baby to cry for long periods or to refuse to settle down at times, if you are at all concerned about his health or well-being, you should always seek advice from a doctor.

Verbal communication

Your baby began to understand the power of language very early on, and started learning to talk from the day he was born. You will find it hard to resist his early

attempts at conversation, and it can be great fun to repeat his grunts and squeaks back to him. These intimate exchanges play an important role. They teach your baby the rudiments of language and conversation, and are vital to the bonding process.

Learning language

From the moment he sets eyes on you, your baby will watch your facial expressions intently and listen to the sounds you make when you talk to him. He will quickly learn to imitate them by moving his lips or muscles as if responding to your words. Listening and imitating are the two main ways in which he picks up language, and he is perfectly designed to do both.

By two or three months, his skills will have already developed to such an extent that he may even start to make his first sounds, cooing when you talk to him or to get your attention. When you coo back to him, imitating his sounds in a two-way "conversation," you are showing him the power of verbal communication, as well as how good it is to express himself.

By five or six months, his imitation skills mean he can babble whole "sentences." And by six months he may have learned to use consonants formed by putting his lips together. He may draw out these sounds to form "maa" and "daa" and will use tone as a means of communicating his mood – shouting out sounds or trilling when he's happy.

Helping him to learn to talk

The more you engage your baby in conversation, the more you will help him to use words to express himself. There are many ways of doing this (and you may find you do most of them automatically). Here are a few suggestions you might like to try.

● **Make lots of eye contact with him when you talk to him,** so that he knows your words are meant for him.

Being face to face also lets him watch how you make sounds with your mouth.

- **Include him and encourage him to participate in your conversations.** When you talk to him, leave time for him to "reply" to you. This may take a few seconds or even longer, so be patient.

- **Talk to him as often as possible.** Describe your actions as you go about your daily chores – say things like, "I'm putting you in the carriage now," for example, to help him to match familiar objects with words.

- **Keep background noise to a minimum.** Switch off the television or radio so that you can give each other your full attention.

- **Repeat things to him as often as possible.** Babies love repetition, and need to hear a word many times before they can begin to understand what it means.

- **Sing nursery rhymes or simple poems over and over again.** This familiarizes him with the rhythms of language by making it fun.

- **Relax.** Learning to talk is a natural outcome of everyday interaction between you, so don't get too hung up about it!

The importance of reading

Up to three months

Reading books to your baby is a great way of interacting with your baby, while familiarizing him with everyday language. It's never too early to make this special time with your baby. Choose board books with big bold pictures in, and without too much background detail.

As his focus develops over the first eight weeks, he will be able to take in more and more. He will love looking at photos or drawings of other babies, and faces will really grab his attention, especially if they have big eyes and smiles. Point to the pictures and talk about them as you go. Encourage other family members to do the same.

Three to six months

Once his focus is perfected and he begins to understand and make more sounds, introduce books that have slightly more detail. Books with simple shapes, colors, and pictures of everyday objects, such as animals or flowers, will be of particular interest. Read him stories if you like – he'll love listening to the tones and rhythms of your voice, while sitting snugly in your lap.

Look for soft or textured books that have pages that feel different – he'll love to handle and explore them. You could also invest in a plastic book that he can enjoy looking at in the bath.

Feeding your baby

Feeding your baby will take up a lot of your time but it can be a great way for you and your baby to bond and enjoy each other. Your breast milk provides her with all her nutritional needs for healthy growth and development. Around four to six months she will have probably doubled her birth weight and will need more solid, nutrient-rich food to fuel her growing energy needs.

Breast-feeding

Breast milk is very easy for your baby to digest and absorb, and has very little "waste." It is much easier for your baby to absorb than formula. And the composition of breast milk adapts constantly to suit your baby's ever-changing needs: your breast milk is very different when your baby is newborn to when she is six months old.

The first "milk" your baby receives after birth is colostrum, a yellow, creamy substance that is high in antibodies, vitamins, and proteins.

After three or four days your breast milk will come in. At the beginning of each feeding your baby will gulp down the thirst-quenching foremilk. This is high in lactose (milk sugar) but low in fat. Once her thirst has been met, her sucking will change to a slow, rhythmic action, as the fat-rich hindmilk comes in. A special enzyme in the milk enables the fat – essential for healthy growth – to be absorbed in your baby's system.

Health benefits

Breast milk far outstrips formula in its nutritional content – it contains more than 100 ingredients that are not found in cow's milk, for example, and which can't be made in a factory. Because it is abundant in antibodies, it is extremely beneficial to your baby's immune system, and provides protection against a whole range of illnesses, including stomach, ear, and respiratory infections. It is also believed to protect against allergy-related conditions, such as asthma and eczema, and against childhood diabetes and some forms of cancer.

Getting started

Breast-feeding is a very rewarding experience. However, some mothers find it difficult to establish breast-feeding to begin with. Your baby may take time latching on, or want to feed all the time, giving you sore nipples and making you worry that you cannot satisfy her. Or your breasts may become "engorged" with milk. Try to get plenty of rest, drink more fluids than usual, and eat healthily. Most first-time mothers do manage to overcome these early problems and go on to enjoy breast-feeding their baby for months.

If you have any concerns about breast-feeding, talk to your doctor or a breast-feeding counsellor. They will be able to offer you support, encouragement, and professional advice.

How your baby feeds

If you stroke your baby's lower lip or cheek with your nipple or a bottle nipple, she will instinctively open her mouth wide and try to take it into her mouth and begin to suck. This is called "rooting." She has been practicing sucking for some time - while she was in your womb she sucked on her hands and fingers. However, this does not mean that feeding her will necessarily be easy at first. Learning to feed - whether from the nipple or the bottle - can take time to perfect, and it may take several days or even weeks before you are both happy with your techniques.

The benefits of expressing

Expressing and storing your breast milk gives you flexibility without reducing your milk flow. It enables someone else to feed your baby sometimes, either simply because they would like to, or to give you a break once in a while. This allows your baby to continue to enjoy the benefits of breast milk for a period after you have gone back to work.

Just because you're breast-feeding, it does not mean that your partner or other caregiver cannot feed your baby whenever it suits. There are a variety of pumps available to buy or rent, enabling you to express some of your milk into a bottle. You can then store the milk in the fridge (if you are planning to use it within 24 hours), or in the freezer for future use.

Bottle-feeding

For those moms who do not breast-feed, years of scientific research have produced formula milks that meet your baby's requirements. Most of these are made from cow's milk with modified protein, carbohydrate, fat,

and added vitamins and minerals that contain a ratio of the proteins similar to those found in breast milk. Some also contain added long-chain fatty acids, although not in their natural form.

● Cow's milk alone is not recommended for babies under one year, since the high protein and salt levels are not easily digestible, and it is low in vitamin C and iron, which is necessary for healthy growth. However, cow's milk can be mixed with your baby's first food, such as baby rice, from six months.

● There are also soy-based formulas, which are made from soy plant protein modified with vitamins and minerals. Soy-based formula milks are often used as an alternative to regular formula milks if your baby suffers from intolerance to cow's milk protein, which affects two per cent of infants.

If your baby is bottle-fed, one of the most obvious benefits is that you can share feeding with your partner or other family members and caregivers.

When to start solid food

Introducing solids is a major milestone in your baby's development. Your baby is not physically able to cope with solid food before she is four months old. Her digestive system is too immature to deal with breaking down food, and she doesn't have the muscular control in her jaws to move food from the front to the back of the mouth until this time. Her kidneys are not yet ready to process food, either.

Your baby is unique and will only be ready to move on to solids at her own pace, but you should offer her first food somewhere between four and six months. Look for signs that she is ready. If she is over four months old and seems to be hungrier than usual, wakes more often during the night, gets excited when she sees others eating or has food near her or tries to grab it, she may be trying to tell you something. Sometimes, babies who are ready to be weaned stop putting on weight too.

Taking it slowly

For the first two weeks just a teaspoon or two of smooth fruit purée, such as apple or pear, and/or baby rice once a day will be all she needs. At this stage you are introducing her to new tastes and consistency, and getting her used to having something slightly more solid in her mouth. If she is too hungry, she won't have the inclination or patience to try solids, so choose a quiet time in between feedings. Don't force her to take the food - mealtimes should be fun, not a trial.

Gradually increase the amount of solid food until you are giving her solids three times a day. At the same time gradually increase the lumpiness of the purées. Avoid giving her wheat-based foods, milk (other than breast or formula), nuts, eggs, citrus fruits, fatty foods, or spices before she is six months old. These may upset your baby's stomach or trigger an allergy if given too early.

Although starting to introduce your baby to solids is exciting, it can be extremely frustrating. This is the first time that she will try food other than milk, experiencing new tastes and textures, and it may take a while for her to get used to solids. At first she will just learn to suck from a spoon, but as she gets on to more lumpy food,

Teething and feeding

Although most babies don't cut their first teeth until at least six months, a few babies begin earlier. Teething may make her irritable and her feeding will become erratic. She may appear to want to suck at the bottle or breast all the time, only to reject it soon afterward because it is so uncomfortable. She may not express any interest in solid food, either.

Her appetite will pick up once the tooth has come through, but if your baby refuses all food (including her regular milk) for more than a day or so, call a doctor to make sure she is not ill.

she will soon start to use her gums to mash it up. Weaning takes a lot of time and patience and, in the beginning, more food will end up smeared around her face or on the floor than in her mouth. Don't worry about how little your baby gets into her mouth - her milk will be her main source of nutrition for some time to come yet.

Eating and social skills

Eating is a very social habit, and as she learns to sit up she can begin to join in family mealtimes. These will also provide a chance for her to develop her personality as she discovers and expresses her likes and dislikes.

Your baby is an able copycat. She will watch you eat, and try to mimic you, picking up a spoon or zwieback and guiding it to her mouth by herself. Although messy, allowing her to experiment like this is important, because it represents a leap forward on the road to independence. It also helps sharpen her hand–eye coordination.

Research shows that good eating habits start young. So, avoid giving your baby food with added sugar, as this is likely to give her a taste for sweet things, which may cause tooth decay later.

Sleeping

Sleep is fundamental to your baby's development. His brain is incredibly active during the early months, growing and making new connections at an amazing rate. He is taking in new information about his world all the time, and while he sleeps this information is being processed and stored for future reference. His body also needs rest in order to store energy, gain strength, and grow.

How much sleep does your baby need?

Your new baby gets exactly the amount of sleep his body needs – he will "shut down" when his body needs to rest or when his brain has had enough stimulation, and he will wake up when he has had enough sleep. To begin with, there is nothing he – or you – can do to control this. He is physiologically designed to shut down and wake up as necessary.

During his first few weeks, he will feed and sleep at regular intervals throughout the day and night. Because he will sleep in relatively short stretches to begin with, you will probably feel quite exhausted – but keep in mind that as he grows he will be able to sleep for longer periods at a time.

It is very hard to predict when and for how long your baby will sleep. On average, a newborn will spend around 16 hours a day sleeping. As he develops, this will gradually decrease, so that at six months he will probably sleep for around 14 hours a day and spend much longer stretches of time awake.

Although newborn babies will drop off at any point of the day or night whenever they need to sleep, by the age of six months your baby will fight to keep himself awake if there is something amusing or stimulating him.

What happens while he is sleeping

It may not look like it, but your baby is doing a lot while he sleeps. His body will be storing the calories he's gained from your milk and converting them into energy for growth and warmth. All the cells in his body and brain are multiplying at a rapid rate, and he is also making white blood cells, which are essential for his immune system. This is also the time when he does most of his growing, since sleep stimulates his growth hormones. Your baby's brain is also very active during sleep.

Your baby's sleep cycle is much shorter than yours – 47 minutes for a newborn compared with 90 minutes for an adult. During this cycle he also spends more time (about 50 percent) in the lighter REM (rapid eye movement) phase of sleep than adults. During these phases his body twitches and his eyelids flicker, indicating that he is dreaming. He is more likely to wake up during these periods. The rest of the time is spent in non-REM sleep – a more peaceful sleep that deepens in four stages, and from which it is difficult to wake.

Developing a sleep pattern

From around four to five weeks, with your help, your baby will start to develop a pattern of sleeping more at night than during the day, which becomes more established over the next few months. At the moment, he cannot differentiate between day and night, so you need to help him learn this.

You can help begin to establish a day/night pattern by putting him to sleep during the day in a room which is not too dark, and where he can hear normal daily sounds, such as the phone ringing, the vacuum cleaner, or people talking. Then, at night, put him to sleep in a different room, which is dark and quiet.

Once your baby is around two months old, you can begin to lay the foundations for a sleep routine. Put him down for his daytime naps at roughly the same time every day – probably during mid-morning and mid-afternoon – and put him to bed at the same time every night. This helps teach your baby that life has a rhythm to it, and instills a sense of security and confidence in

himself and his environment. By six months, he may be sleeping for around ten consecutive hours at night and five non-consecutive hours during his daytime naps.

Establishing a bedtime routine

As he becomes more aware of what's going on around him and his memory skills improve, your baby will learn to anticipate events and familiarize himself with the patterns of his days. He will probably respond very well to routine at this stage, and start to enjoy the rituals of preparing for his nighttime sleep. Try to follow the same pattern at around the same time every evening. For example, you could start off with a warm bath, followed by cuddling and gentle play. You could then feed him and put him into his crib, drowsy but awake, perhaps accompanied by a lullaby.

Putting your baby down to sleep while he is still awake means that he won't depend on your breast or the bottle in order to fall asleep. It also means that if he stirs he will know where he is and may feel secure enough to drop off again without disturbing you, unless he is hungry or uncomfortable.

If possible, involve your partner in your baby's bedtime routine. Perhaps he could bathe him or read a book with him. It will strengthen the bond between them, and help to build up trust, so that your baby won't rely solely on you for his sense of security and well-being.

Sleeping with your baby

Close proximity to your baby is important during the early months, not least because you will have to feed him frequently at night. You may find that you want to have your baby in bed with you, especially if you are breast-feeding. Some studies have shown that co-sleeping is beneficial for your baby; it may help regulate his breathing and body temperature, for example, and there is also evidence to suggest that it can be good for your baby's emotional development. The feeling of having him close to you can be wonderful, and may also decrease your anxiety about his well-being.

Whether you sleep with your baby is a very personal choice. Parents in many cultures do so intuitively, but this does not mean that you will. It is important that both you and your baby have periods of restful sleep. If you try having your baby in bed with you, and find that you and your partner are uncomfortable, then placing the baby in a crib is probably the best option for your family.

Why does he keep waking up?

During your baby's first six months, his sleep patterns are bound to change. He may sleep for five hours at a time for a few weeks, and then suddenly start waking up every two hours, for instance. Sleep during the first six months is linked with his feeding requirements: he may be having a growth spurt, for example, and need more milk to be sustained. Erratic sleep patterns are normal, and sticking to a routine will help you both get through these difficult times. Many babies don't sleep through the night regularly until they are six months old or more.

Important safety tips

SIDS

All parents worry about the possibility of crib death, technically known as Sudden Infant Death Syndrome (SIDS). Although the chances of this happening to your baby are remote, it is sensible to take a few simple precautions that are known to reduce the risk.

★ Put your baby down to sleep on his back with his feet at the foot of the crib.

★ Use loose blankets and sheets.

★ Do not use crib bumpers.

★ Never use a hot-water bottle or an electric blanket.

★ Do not give him a pillow.

★ Use a firm mattress, and make sure there's no gap between the edges and the sides of the crib.

★ Never smoke around your baby, and keep him away from smoky atmospheres.

★ Make sure your baby's bedroom is not overheated and avoid overbundling your baby in night clothing. The temperature of your baby's bedroom should be comfortable for a lightly clothed adult. Overheating can be life-threatening because your baby's body is not mature enough to deal with the excess heat by sweating. This is believed to be one of the primary causes of crib death.

Considerations when co-sleeping

If you have your baby in the bed with you, there are several things that you need to keep in mind to make sure that he is safe and comfortable.

First you will want to ensure that there is adequate space in the bed for the baby. If the bed is too cramped, he can become overheated or you might crowd or roll over on him. Never give your baby a pillow or cover him with a comforter.

It's also important that you and your partner are alert and attentive to the baby's needs. Therefore, you should avoid having him in bed with you if you are overly tired, taking a medication that makes you drowsy, or have recently consumed alcoholic beverages.

Coping with broken nights is hard work, but your baby is waking up for a number of reasons. In the early days, his stomach is so small that it can only hold tiny amounts of milk that won't keep him going through the night, so hunger wakes him. Other factors can also affect his sleep. He may have tummy ache, or a soiled diaper or teething pains, for example, all of which can cause enough discomfort to wake him. A blocked nose causes difficulties, too, since babies only learn to breathe through their mouths at two to three months old. Reaching a new developmental milestone can also affect sleeping patterns. For example, it is thought that the mental stimulation from learning to sit up or crawl at around five to six months may be enough to disturb a baby's sleep, although other theories say that this can actually make the baby sleep for longer periods.

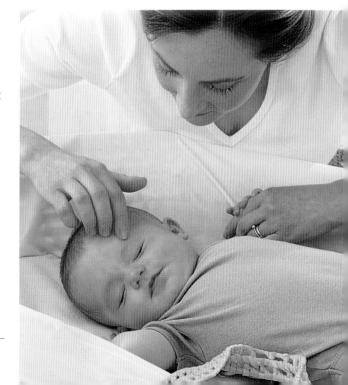

Checkups and charts

Regular development checkups with your doctor or healthcare professional will reassure you that your baby is doing well and provide an opportunity for you to talk about the practical aspects of parenting as well as any anxieties you may have about your baby's development.

Development reviews

Checkups to assess your baby's development will take place at various intervals during the first few years of your baby's life. The results, along with a record of

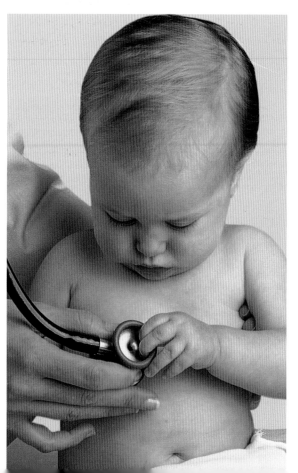

which immunizations your baby has had, are recorded in your child's medical records. The stage at which reviews are done varies, but, as a general guide, you can expect one at around six to eight weeks, then one at four months, six months, nine months, and 12 months.

The six-week development checkup

The six-week checkup is primarily concerned with your baby's physical health and how she is feeding, as well as her overall development.

This check is quite informal and will not be the same for every baby in every area. Normally, your baby's weight, head circumference, and sometimes her length will be noted. You will be asked to undress your baby to do these measurements, and her hips may be checked too, as occasionally dislocation is not picked up at the newborn check.

The doctor may then listen to your baby's heart and lungs with a stethoscope and look into her eyes with a hand-held light (ophthalmoscope). She may also check your baby's ears and mouth for infection.

Many of the reflexes she was born with, such as the grasp reflex, should have disappeared by now, and your doctor will probably test these. Your baby's growing head control will be assessed, too, because it is an important developmental pointer. Her motor

development begins at the head and travels down through her trunk, arms and legs (so, as unlikely as it sounds, being able to hold her head up is the first step to learning to walk).

Questions you may be asked

You may find that when your baby is being examined, the doctor or healthcare professional does not formally "test" your baby but instead asks you questions about her. These may include:

- how your baby is feeding
- whether you have any concerns about her hearing
- whether she watches your face or follows moving objects with her eyes
- whether she smiles at you
- whether she is startled by loud noises.

You may also be asked some questions about how you are coping, because the key to her healthy development is in her relationships with you and her immediate family. Your doctor will also probably want to book your baby's first immunizations, which occur at around six weeks and at two, four, and six months.

Growth and height charts

Recording how much your baby weighs and measures can provide a very useful guide to the general progress and development of your baby.

Weight gain varies considerably between babies, but on average they gain around 4–6oz (100–175g) per week for the first few weeks of life (although immediately after the birth, her weight will probably take a dip first). After this, the average baby gains between 1 and 2lb (450 and 900g) until she is around six months of age. Weight gain is usually quickest in the first six to nine months.

If you take your baby to be weighed every week, you will probably find that some weeks she has gained weight and others she hasn't. This is perfectly normal. What is important is her general weight gain over a period of weeks, which is measured against a percentile chart. Some doctors will measure against a percentile chart that is not only appropriate to the gender of the baby but also to her racial origins.

Percentile charts

Every percentile chart has a "middle line" plotted on it. This represents the national average. For example, if 100 babies were weighed at the same age, 50 will weigh more than the amount indicated by the line, and 50 will weigh less.

★ Most babies will fall somewhere in the shaded areas of the chart, although around four percent may fall outside these percentiles. Boys and girls have different charts because boys are on average heavier and taller, and their growth pattern is slightly different.

★ Whatever weight your baby is at birth, she should have a fairly steady growth, resulting in a line curving in roughly the same way. If it suddenly drops or climbs severely out of this range, it can occasionally indicate a problem – an illness or feeding difficulties, for example.

Developing good health

Your baby's health is intricately linked with his emotional well-being and general development. By nurturing him and responding to his needs, you are ensuring that he will develop into a happy and a healthy baby. Touching and caressing your baby regularly helps everything from cell regeneration to digestion. Making sure that he is not distressed or uncomfortable will help promote healthy growth and development.

Boosting your baby's health

To maximize your baby's health, try to do the following:

● **Breast-feed him.** This gives him the healthiest possible start in life, since your breast milk contains antibodies that protect him from harmful diseases in the early months and boost his immune system.

● **Don't smoke around him.** By keeping him away from polluted atmospheres, you will reduce the chances of his getting respiratory diseases or allergies such as asthma.

● **Avoid introducing solid food too early.** Before he is four months old, his digestive system is not mature enough to cope with anything other than breast milk or formula. Introducing solids too early could damage his kidneys and may increase the risk of developing allergies.

● **Take him to the doctor regularly,** and make sure you don't miss his reviews.

● Discuss when and how to get your baby **immunized** with your doctor or healthcare professional.

Immunization

When your baby is around eight weeks old, you will probably be asked to take him for the first of several immunizations. When your baby is immunized, he is given a vaccine that contains harmless amounts of the virus that causes the disease. This makes your baby's body produce antibodies, which will protect him from developing the disease in the future. Your baby may develop a mild fever afterward, and may have a small, hard lump at the site of the injection. This will last a few weeks and is nothing to worry about.

Vaccine	To protect against	Age usually given	Method
DTaP	Diphtheria, tetanus, pertussis	Two, four and six months	Injection
PV	Polio	Two, four, and six months	Injection or oral drops
Hib	Haemophilus influenzae type B	Two, four, and six months	Injection
Hep B	Hepatitis B (if mother is negative)	Two, three, and six months	Injection
Pneumococcal (PVC)	Pneumococcal disease	Two, four, and six months	Injection

Credit: American Academy of Pediatrics. Recommmended childhood immunization schedule, United States, January–December 2001

How babies learn

The first six months of your baby's life will be an incredible learning experience for you both. You'll soon become the world's expert on your baby – and she'll get to know you pretty well, too! During this time, your newborn will develop into a confident person who has learned a lot about herself, her environment, and how to relate to the people around her.

How babies learn skills

Each time you pick him up, play with him, talk or sing to him, cuddle him, smile at him, or soothe him, you are giving your baby information about his world and what it means to be a human being. Above all, you are teaching him that he is loved. This security gives him confidence to explore his environment, developing new skills on the way, mainly by watching and copying you.

As the weeks and months pass, your baby will enthral and impress you with a dazzling array of new skills. He will gain control over his own body, and learn that he can control his environment (by picking up toys, or kicking at his mobile to make it move, for example). He will respond to you with real excitement, communicate his needs and desires, and know just how to make you laugh. He will become well attuned to the sounds, rhythms, and tones of language and will love to practice his own. He will be fascinated by his environment, and actively participate in everything going on around him. Best of all, your baby will become adept at expressing real pleasure in life – smiling, gurgling, cooing – and he will know just how to make you feel this pleasure, too.

How to help him learn

Being your baby's "teacher" doesn't mean you have to give him constant stimulation and surround him with all the latest toys. "Playing" with your baby during these early months is about giving him your attention when he wants it. Research shows that parents tend to do this naturally, but here are some pointers on how to help him get the best out of his developing awareness.

● Stimulate his senses. Before he can move around independently, your baby explores the world with his five senses – sight, touch, taste, hearing, and smell.

● Face him. He needs lots of eye-to-eye contact to learn to communicate effectively and to feel secure.

● Get him involved. Point out things, describe them, and talk to him all the time. By doing this, you are helping him pick up language as well as stimulating his curiosity.

● Repeat yourself. Babies learn by repetition, and you'll help him by repeating words to promote recognition.

● Take his lead. Don't push your baby to play if he's not in the mood – learn to read his cues.

FASCINATION WITH HANDS
This two-month-old baby has discovered her hands, and spends a lot of time watching them. She is fascinated by the noises the brightly colored wrist toy makes as she moves her hand.

- Act it out. Describe and demonstrate whatever you are saying or doing. Babies really respond to exaggerated expressions.
- Entertain him. Play new games, think of new songs, and give him new experiences when you can, so he doesn't get bored.
- Respond to him. If he cries, cuddle him. If he laughs, laugh with him. Acknowledge how he's feeling.
- Tell him he's fantastic. Just like adults, babies love to be encouraged and told how clever they are.

0–6 months: your baby's milestones

The following is a very rough guide to which skills your baby is likely to develop, and when. Remember that there is a wide variation of what's normal for each month.

The first month
- recognizes your voice and smell
- may try to lift his head when on his tummy
- sticks his tongue out in response to you doing it

The second month
- moves his head from side to side
- smiles for the first time
- coos in response to you
- loses some newborn reflexes
- makes smoother movements

HAND–EYE COORDINATION
This six-month-old has no trouble swiping at the tower of bricks her mother has carefully built, successfully knocking it over.

- shows excitement when he knows you are near
- can see things farther away
- opens and closes mouth in imitation of you when you talk to him

The third month
- becomes more interested in people around him
- starts to notice his hands
- can open and close his hands and play with his fingers
- may hold his head for a few seconds
- may push himself up on his arms briefly when lying on his tummy
- clasps a toy in his hand
- swipes at toys
- reaches out and grabs at things
- experiments with vowel sounds
- may gurgle

The fourth month
- head control becomes steady
- uses hands to explore his own face and objects of interest
- may make recognizable sounds
- can remember some things – for example, that a rattle makes a noise

The fifth month
- grabs his toes and puts them in his mouth

- may try to take his weight on his legs when held upright
- starts rolling over from front to back
- turns his head away when he doesn't want any more food
- reaches for toys he wants
- concentrates for short periods
- puts everything in his mouth
- raises his arms to be picked up
- wants to be included in everything
- becomes excited at the prospect of food

The sixth month
- holds head steady
- grasps objects
- enjoys sitting up with support
- starts to chuckle
- blows bubbles and raspberries
- changes tone of voice to express himself
- initiates interaction by getting your attention by making sounds and banging objects

Birth to 1 month

It may seem to you that all your newborn does is eat, sleep, and cry – but from the moment she is born, she is developing new skills with incredible speed. By the end of her first month, she will have become more alert and responsive, started to gain some bodily control and coordination, learned to recognize you when she sees or hears you, and has even begun to respond to you.

Physical development

During the early weeks, your baby will still be curled up, with her legs drawn in and her hands clenched, but it will not be long before her body begins to stretch out as her joints become less flexed. Make sure that you always support her head, and never shake her.

Movement

Even before she was born, your baby was exercising her muscles – and now she has a lot more space to do it in. When she is alert, she will punch the air and kick her legs vigorously, especially in response to stimulation or when she is agitated or crying. These movements are jerky, random, and uncontrolled at the moment, but they strengthen her muscles and stimulate her nervous system, paving the way for more controlled attempts later on.

If you lay your baby on her tummy or hold her in the air face down, she will probably try to lift her head. Letting her do this now and again will help strengthen her neck, chest, and spine muscles.

Learning skills

Your baby is learning all the time – and the main way she does this is through her relationship with you.

She is incredibly receptive to any kind of contact you have with her: notice how she becomes still and concentrates when she hears your voice, or how she watches your moving lips with fascination as you talk to her. Watch her carefully and you may see her move her body in excitement when she knows you are near. She is deriving enormous pleasure from this relationship, and her brain is being stimulated, too.

Senses

Your baby's senses are exquisitely attuned to help her to take in all the information she needs for survival and development. For instance, she can recognize your unique smell just hours after birth, and she will quickly learn to associate it with the sound of your voice and the comforting feeling of being held in your arms.

Seeing clearly

At birth, your baby can only see the edges of things, because the center of her visual field is still blurred. During the first month, however, she will gradually acquire the ability to focus better – although full "binocular" vision won't come until she's around three months old.

At the moment, your baby will focus best at around 8–15in (20–35cm) – just the right distance

Head control

Before your baby can control her body, she needs to master the art of holding her head unsupported.

To begin with, her head will be very floppy because it is so heavy, but over the next few weeks her neck muscles and the muscles at the top of her spine will gradually strengthen, allowing her to support her head herself.

Until she has full head control – which may not come until she is four months old – you must always make sure you support her head when you are holding her.

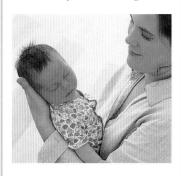

for scanning your face when you are feeding and holding her. At this distance, your baby will be able to follow your face as it moves.

Focusing on your face and those of your family is crucial to your baby. But it is also useful to suspend a mobile above her crib (slightly to one side), so that the images on the mobile are roughly this distance away from her face but not immediately above it.

Language

Even at this stage, your baby is tuning into the tones and rhythms of language all the time. Talk to your baby as much as you can, and try to use exaggerated modulation in your speech. It's OK to use "baby talk" at this stage of her development. You are beginning to teach her the building blocks of conversation.

It won't be long before she starts to respond to you, by making little noises or moving her mouth.

Emotional and social development

Your newborn is a little bundle of emotions. From the first few moments of life, she is very sensitive to the moods and feelings of the people she is close to – for example, she may become agitated if you are feeling upset or worried, and seem more calm and content when you are feeling relaxed. This emotional sensitivity is an important newborn characteristic.

In later stages of development, it will help her adjust her behavior and

Activities to develop skills

At this age your baby has all the toys she needs rolled into one – you! You are the most fascinating thing to her, and will be for some time yet. Your face is the most captivating thing of all. Let her enjoy you as you make different expressions, talk, and sing to her. Encourage your partner and other members of the family to interact with her, too, by making different facial expressions and sounds.

Copy cat!

Try sticking your tongue out at your baby every 20 seconds when she is looking into your eyes, and you may soon see a tiny tongue sticking back at you. Be patient – it may take a minute or two before she responds.

Tracking games

Sound and motion attract your baby's attention and will help stimulate her brain. To help sharpen her visual skills, get her to follow your face with her eyes. Move your head slowly from side to side as you hold her facing you, and see if she "tracks" you with her eyes.

Light and shade

Your baby's attention will be caught by objects with bold patterns of light and shade: your face, a Venetian

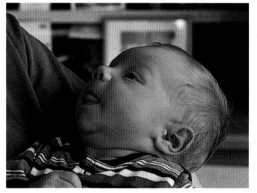

MY TURN
After watching his father stick out his tongue at him several times, this baby is delighted to find that he can do it, too.

blind, or a black-and-white picture, for example. This is because strong contrasts are easily picked out even with poor vision.

★ Draw some black-and-white patterns and faces and stick them on to the wall by her crib.

★ Lie her by a window where there is a play of light and shade, perhaps caused by foliage outside.

★ Place her carriage under a tree with low branches and let her enjoy the changes in light and shade.

Sense of touch

Splash water in the bath with her feet while you hold her carefully supported in your arm. This will stimulate her sense of touch without making her feel insecure.

respond appropriately to the people around her. In other words, your baby's awareness of the moods and feelings of others is fundamental to her development into a "social" human being.

You will probably find that, to begin with, it is hard to fathom exactly how your baby is feeling or what it is she needs or wants. But as your relationship develops, she will become easier to read, and both you and your baby will find the time you spend together increasingly emotionally rewarding.

Crying

For now, your baby's physical requirements take priority over everything, and she will express herself accordingly. She will cry to express hunger, fatigue, or discomfort, and sometimes she will cry because she is bored and in need of stimulation, or feeling vulnerable and in need of cuddling.

Respond to your baby's cries and give her all the reassurance she needs. Lots of attention and love now will teach her how to respond positively to you, and will help her develop into a secure and confident baby.

Happiness

You will be able to tell when your baby is feeling happy or content because she will lie peacefully,

Toy box

Mobiles

For newborns, a mobile with bold black-and-white faces or patterns on it is ideal. Simple, colorful shapes will also catch her interest, and musical mobiles that go around will fascinate her and help her develop her "tracking" skills.

Hang the mobile to one side of her crib rather than directly above her – newborns rarely look straight ahead; they spend most of their time looking to their right or left in the early weeks. Don't worry if she doesn't appear interested in it at first; many babies don't take any notice until later.

Mirrors

Put a baby-safe mirror in the crib so that she can see her own face. This will help her focus, and reinforce her inborn response to the human face.

Music tapes

Whether it's Chopin or "Hey Diddle Diddle," your baby will pick up the rhythms, melodies, and repetition.

Test her memory by playing the same music over several days. Then leave it for a day or two before repeating the same music, and see if she recognizes it. You'll know if she remembers it because she'll kick or suddenly become more alert.

looking intently into your eyes or at her surroundings. These moments may be short-lived to begin with, because most of her time will be spent feeding or sleeping, but they will be very pleasurable for you both when they do occur.

Quiet, content times are very important for your baby for many reasons. They give her the chance to let her physical needs take a back seat for a while, and her brain can take over. This means she can exercise her curiosity, practice focusing on things, and, most

important of all, give you some undivided attention. And just being with you will make her feel secure and happy. These periods when your baby is quiet yet alert are some of the special moments when you and your baby can really get to know one another.

Knowing that your baby is content can be incredibly emotionally fulfilling – it is a sign that you are meeting her needs. This will increase your confidence as a parent, and, at the same time, strengthen your bond with your baby.

1 to 2 months

By the end of the second month, your newborn will have developed into a baby with an intense interest in what's going on around him, as well as more control over his body. At about six weeks old, he will also start to reward your affection with spontaneous smiles, and his personality will really begin to shine through.

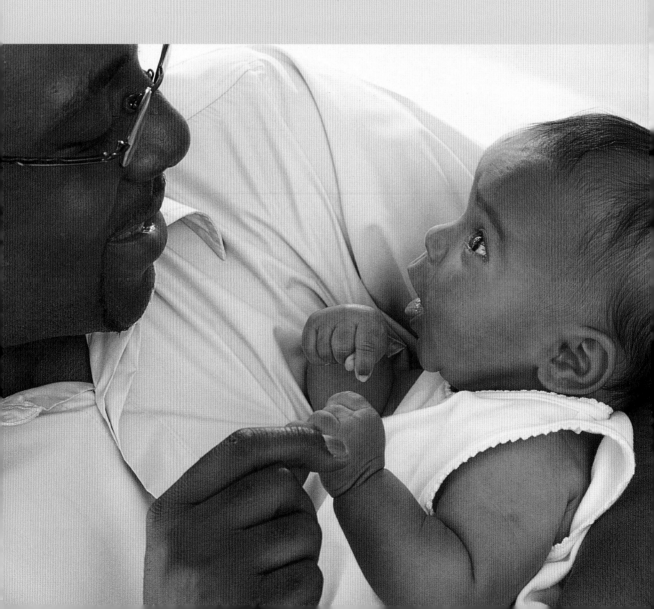

Physical development

Your baby is rapidly growing in size and strength. His muscles are getting stronger, his movements are becoming more definite, and, by eight weeks, he is already far less vulnerable than he was at birth. He will also lose many of his newborn reflexes at this stage.

Uncurling

Your baby will now begin to stretch out and uncurl from his fetal position. His knees and hips will be stronger, and they won't be as flexed as before. And the tightly clenched fingers of your newborn will unfold one by one into an open hand, ready for clasping objects.

By the end of this month, if you put a rattle into his palm, he will probably be able to grasp it automatically and to hold on to it for a little while.

Head control

He will now make more attempts to lift his head, and may be able to raise it to an angle of as much as 45 degrees for a second or two when lying on his tummy. This ability is a sign that his neck muscles are becoming stronger.

He will also turn his head when he wants to – for example, if his interest is attracted by a sudden or new

First smile

Your baby's first true smile will probably appear at around six weeks. You can tell it's a real smile, because his eyes light up at the same time, and, as you respond by smiling back, it becomes stronger. Although he may have made previous practice runs during the early weeks of his life, you'll recognize the real thing because he'll use his whole face, especially his eyes.

This is a real breakthrough in his development. The more he smiles at you, the more you will smile back and talk to him. His happy face cannot help but engage you in interaction with him, and this is exactly what he needs to develop into a social human being.

Once he has learned to smile, there will be no stopping him. He will probably smile at anyone he sees to begin with, especially if someone is looking at him and talking to him. But within just a few weeks, you will notice that he is a lot more choosy about who he really smiles at; he

will quickly learn to tell the difference between familiar faces and strange ones, saving his most meaningful smiles for the faces he loves most of all.

More than anything else, this is a thoroughly enjoyable stage in your baby's development. His smile is telling you that he is happy – so smile back at him and let him know you're happy, too!

RESPONDING TO YOU
Your baby's first smile will come in direct response to you or your partner's smiling at him.

sound or image, or simply when he hears the sound of your voice.

Movement

Those funny jerky kicks of the first few weeks will now become smoother, like pedaling actions. He will spend more time awake now, and a lot of his alert periods will be taken up by exercising his limbs and punching out with his arms, which

are also gaining in strength. He will probably take more interest in his mobile. You could also try putting him under a baby gym on the floor, so that he has something to swipe at. He will miss most of the time to begin with, because, even though his arm movements are becoming more purposeful, his coordination and his ability to judge the distance between objects is still quite poor at this age.

Learning skills

Your baby will now take an interest in his surroundings. It will be very clear that he recognizes you. He will start to show his excitement when he sees you by jerking his whole body with pleasure, kicking and waving his legs and arms. You'll notice now that he looks in the direction of any sounds and movements, and he may also follow you with his eyes as you move around nearby.

Vision and sound

During this month, your baby will practice focusing both eyes on the same point at the same time. (This is known as binocular vision.) He will soon be able to scan faces more broadly than before, noticing the

Activities to develop skills

You are still your baby's number-one favorite play thing. Talk to him, rock him, sing to him, or put on some music or sing a lullabye and dance around the room with him – all these activities will bring him pleasure and stimulate him, with positive results. Sing to him as you bathe him: gently splash water over his toes and tummy as you support his body in the water.

Sensory stimulation

★ Prop him up in a car seat or a bouncer seat, so that he gets a good view of what's going on around him. Talk to him from different places in the room and watch how he tries to locate the sound. Games like this help him to coordinate sight and sound.

★ Play "This Little Piggy" with his hands and feet to encourage his fingers and toes to relax. Open out his fingers or toes as you say the rhyme. This will also reinforce your baby's ideas about enjoyment and interaction.

★ Repeat the same song a few times, and see how long it takes before he learns to anticipate the tickle at the end.

★ Your baby will also love it if you tickle the palm of his hand and his fingertips with anything soft or furry in texture.

1 *Supporting this baby carefully with his body, her father begins to play "This Little Piggy" with the toes of her right foot. She does not know what to expect yet, and looks slightly skeptical!*

2 *The second time he goes through the sequence, she knows what is going to happen next. Her smiling face is alight with anticipation at the prospect of the tickling that ends this game.*

details, such as eyes and nose, rather than the overall outlines and contrasts. Your baby will now also be able to see things that are farther away, although he will still prefer to look at things that are close up.

His understanding of language has become more sophisticated, and he may open and close his mouth in imitation of speech when you talk to him. He will also adjust his behavior to the sound of your voice, quieting when you speak soothingly and becoming distressed if he hears rough or loud tones.

Memory

Although your baby's memory is very short-term in the early weeks, his ability to remember is improving and becoming more sophisticated. To help stimulate his memory, let him experience things with more than one sense. For example, he is far more likely to remember a toy if he has been allowed to touch it as well as look at it, because his memory will include details about the toy's shape and texture as well as its outline and color.

Emotional and social development

The lovely thing about this stage in your baby's development is that he is already learning to recognize and

Toy box

Baby gym

A baby gym or cradle gym (one that you hang over a carriage or crib) has an array of interesting objects hanging from it and will keep your baby well entertained. Choose a gym with toys that make a noise as well as those that are colorful. He'll love things that squeak, rustle, or rattle.

A mobile will help his visual development and he will love to practice his swiping skills on it (see p.45). Move his position from time to time so that he can look at all the different toys hanging from it, and frequently change the toys that hang from it to prevent him from getting bored.

Books

It's never too early to introduce your baby to books. Choose board books designed for young babies that have clear, bold pictures of faces, babies, animals, or patterns. They will help your baby familiarize himself with everyday faces and objects. Stand the book up next to him so it's in line with his gaze, and change the pages occasionally. Better still, sit him on your lap and talk about the pictures, pointing things out as you go.

Rattles

He'll love to hold a rattle and enjoy the sound it makes when you shake it for him, even if he can't do much with it himself at the moment.

respond to you. The most rewarding response is the appearance at around six weeks' old of his first real smile (see p.45).

He will still cry, but he is also discovering other ways to get your attention and communicate his feelings, using his whole face and body to get the response he wants.

Learning to be sociable

Your baby will look more intently at faces now because his vision is becoming less blurred, and he'll become more adept at imitating facial gestures. His awareness of what's going on around him means that he is taking in more, picking up more clues about how to interact with you, tuning into the nuances of language, tone, and expression and filing all this new information away for future reference.

Your baby will love any kind of interaction now, and he will adore physical affection, responding warmly to cuddling, rocking, and skin-to-skin contact.

2 to 3 months

Your baby is now stronger and more in control of her movements, and will become more responsive and communicative toward you, using gurgles, sounds, and smiles. By the end of this month, she will be able to hold her head steady, and she will have discovered a source of great pleasure – her hands.

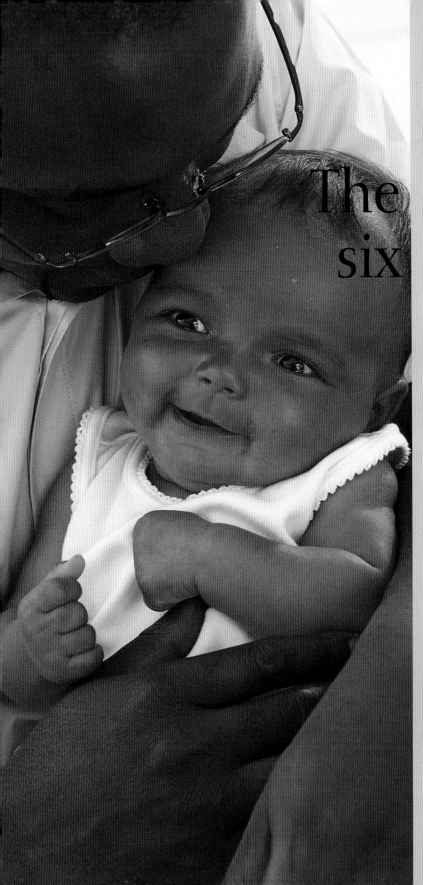

The first six months

When you hold your newborn baby in your arms, it's impossible to imagine him as a strapping six-month old. But it won't be long before he's sitting in a high chair, throwing spoonfuls of fruit puree around, and interacting with the family as though he's always been there. How does your baby cover so much ground in such a short space of time?

Your baby's development

Your baby naturally develops at a quite incredible pace – but at the same time every achievement that he makes, every new milestone that he passes, is intricately bound up with all you do to make sure he is happy, secure, and loved.

The most important point to remember as your baby grows is that babies develop at different rates. Like all babies, your newborn will smile, lift his head, babble, and grab things at specific times – but your baby is also unique. He won't do something just because a book says he will or because you want him to. The "right time" will be when he is ready. Charts and books like this one can only offer general guides to how babies develop. You cannot speed up the developmental timetable, but if you are giving your baby lots of love and care, you are giving him exactly what he needs: the wherewithal to develop at his own pace.

All he needs is love

Your baby's development doesn't happen in isolation from the rest of the world; he can only learn and progress by being part of it. Having you, your partner, siblings, friends, and family members there is fundamental to his learning and developing.

Not only does he learn by example, he needs acknowledgment, love, and encouragement from the people around him in order to reach his full potential. So by doing what comes naturally – cuddling him, talking to him, going to him when he cries, and interacting with him – you are giving him a sense of security and confidence that allows him to blossom.

You are developing, too

As your baby learns to do more and more, your skills as a parent will adapt to meet his new needs. By your baby's four-month birthday, you will probably have established a daily routine for him, revolving around feeding, napping, going for a walk in the park or to stores, bathing, and going to sleep at night. A routine will help you both feel secure and confident, and will provide the foundations of your life together as a family.

The development process

Development is rarely a linear process: occasionally your baby's development may seem to take a step backward. For example, he may have slept through the night for several weeks and then suddenly start waking up every three hours again for no obvious reason.

Such seemingly backward steps are perfectly normal – in fact, they are often a sign that he is about to take a developmental leap forward. You may find that a week or two down the line, he's considerably more alert and responsive to people and events around him, or is sleeping less during the day than before.

Playing is learning

Playing with your baby is not only fun, it provides the fabric of your baby's learning experiences. Every time you play or interact with him, you are not simply entertaining him; you're teaching him invaluable lessons about himself, about you, and about the world.

For example, by shaking a rattle for your new baby, you are helping him learn to focus, as well as introducing him to the concept of cause and effect – after a while he will begin to understand that shaking the rattle is what makes the noise. And by playing "This Little Piggy" on your two-month-old's toes, you are introducing him to the delights of anticipation (in this particular case, the tickle at the end) as well as the nature of counting rhythms. A game of hide the teddy with your five-month-old helps him grasp complex concepts, such as the fact that objects exist even when he cannot see them. Of course, all the time you are playing these simple games with your baby he is developing his own sense of humor, and letting you know just how funny he finds your jokes!

About this book

During these thrilling six months of change, your support, encouragement, and love can do more than anything else to help your baby blossom. But understanding how your baby develops is vital to helping you tune into his needs and give him what he wants.

Section 1

The first half of this book tells you all about how your baby's development will affect both his physical and his emotional needs. For example, why does your five-month-old keep waking at night when he previously slept through? How important is it that he learns to roll over or grab hold of things at a certain age?

Being one step ahead in terms of knowing what to expect from your baby will help you understand him so you can respond in the best and most effective way possible. And being able to meet his needs in this way will not only help him feel loved and valued but boost your confidence as a parent too.

Section 2

The second half of this book contains a wealth of information about how and when your baby is likely to reach each new milestone. Although the information is organized by month, it's important to remember that the time scale is flexible. Babies develop at different rates, and your baby will progress at the speed that's right for him.

Babies' skills, however, progress in a predictable sequence because a certain amount of growth and development has to take place before a new skill can be acquired. So don't expect your baby to sit up without support, for example, before he's strong enough to support his own head.

Once you see your baby trying to do something new, there are lots of things you can do to try to encourage him along the way, and this section includes ideas for games and activities you can play with him. Giving your baby the right kind of stimulation will build his confidence and self-esteem and will help give him the best possible start in life.

The birth

It's hard to say exactly what your baby feels as she is transported from the cosy comfort of the womb into your arms, but if your pregnancy has reached full term she should be well prepared for survival in the outside world.

The effects of birth on your baby

The transition from your womb to the birth room triggers a number of changes in the way your baby's organs function, placing new demands on her body.

The most significant of these is that she now starts to breathe for herself. While in the womb, her lungs were filled with amniotic fluid, but this is usually expelled during labor because of the compression as she passes through the birth canal. This leaves her free to take her first gulp of air, and as she does this her blood circulation will quickly adapt to ensure that there is enough oxygen in her body to cope with life outside the womb.

Babies born by cesarean section sometimes need help to clear their lungs because they haven't been "squeezed out" in the birth canal. The effects of anesthesia can also cause temporary breathing difficulties and, if your baby was born under general anesthetic, she may be as drowsy as you for some hours after the birth.

What is she feeling?

The sudden sense of space and air on your baby's skin will be a shock to her senses, which will have already been highly stimulated by the birth. In fact, newborns are often more alert during the first moments after being born than at any other time during the first few days.

If you are not too exhausted from labor and your baby is alert, take advantage of this special time. She will be very responsive to your touch, voice, and warmth. Stroking her, cuddling her, talking to her, and letting her nurse will facilitate a loving bond between you. These early moments are a wonderful opportunity for you and your baby to get to know each other. But on the other hand don't worry if you don't get the chance to do this immediately: there will be plenty of time in the coming weeks and months.

Birth weight

One of the first questions people ask when a baby is born (after they've asked what sex it is) is: "How much does she weigh?" Birth weight is considered important because it can give a general indication of a baby's vitality, but healthy babies come in all shapes and sizes. A petite baby weighing 6lb 9oz (3kg) can be as vigorous

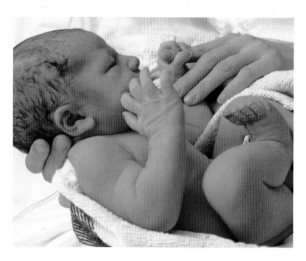

Physical development

As your baby gains control over her body, she will begin to understand how she can use it to learn more about her world.

Pushing up

Her neck muscles will now be so strong that, when she lies on her back, she can lift her head and hold it up for several seconds. When you grasp her hands and pull her to a sitting position, her head may no longer flop back, but will lift up as her body is pulled upward.

Sit her in a bouncer seat or a baby play nest, and she may be able to hold her head steady. Lie her on her stomach and she'll begin doing mini pushups, trying to lift herself with her hands and arms, and turning her head to get a good look at what's around her.

She may not be able to hold these positions for long, but every time she does it her muscles are strengthening. This gives her much more opportunity to take in her surroundings, and she will become increasingly curious about them.

Happy hands

They may have been there all along, but your baby has only just noticed that her hands are there! Her hands will now become an ever-present source of fascination to her, and she will spend a lot of time lying still and intently examining her new-found fingers, watching as they interact with one another.

By the end of this month, she will be able to bring her hands together and play with her fingers, jamming them in her mouth, where she will enjoy sucking them. She will love to watch her hands as they clasp and unclasp, and will press her palms together in a clapping motion.

Learning skills

Your baby is already a keen thinker. She is now fascinated by her own body and is beginning to understand that she can make it move by herself when she wants to. This is an important first step in your baby's understanding of the concept of cause and effect. She is also beginning to connect seeing with doing, which is the first step in developing hand–eye coordination.

Memory

Your baby's memory will now have developed sufficiently for her to remember certain people and events. One study of babies of this age found that they quickly learn how to kick a mobile attached to their crib to make it move.

When the mobile was taken away for a week and then put back in place, the babies could still remember what to do.

Reaching and grabbing

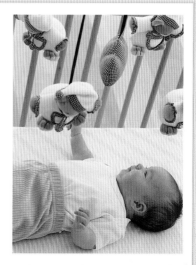

Although she won't be able to reach for things by herself yet, if you hand her a toy she will clasp it for a short time, and may even try to bring it into her line of vision. When she is lying under her mobile or baby gym, she'll now take definite swipes at the toys hanging down, and may succeed in grabbing one.

Notice how she opens and shuts her hand as if to grab the object of her desire. Although she isn't yet coordinated enough to catch it, she will grab at anything that looks tempting and is within her reach.

Language

Your baby will begin to experiment more with vowel sounds, and her vocabulary will range from brief, one-syllable squeaks and squeals to long "eh" and "oh" vowel sounds. She is beginning to discover which sounds are made by which combinations of throat, tongue, and mouth actions.

At first, these cooing, throaty gurgles will seem completely random, but you will gradually notice that the sounds your baby is making are directed at you when you talk to her. She is enjoying socializing with you, as well as the sound of her own voice.

Vision

Your baby's focus will really sharpen now, although she may still work to focus with both eyes properly. She will be able to see more detail in patterns and faces, as well as differences between sharp and gradual changes in lighting. For example, if her room has a dimmer switch, you will be able to attract her attention by changing the lighting.

Toy box

Wrist toys

Now she has found her hands, your baby might enjoy having a wrist toy or bell bracelet Velcroed round her wrist. She'll begin to learn that by shaking it she's making the noise.

Rattles and mobiles

She will like to hold a rattle, and pull at toys hanging from her mobile with more confidence.

Noisy toys

Toys that make a noise, like a squeaky duck, will now be very entertaining. You'll need to help her squeak these for a while, since they may still be too hard for her to manipulate, but she will love the surprise sound they make.

Once she has learned how to make a toy squeak, she'll get even more pleasure from it – and, what is more, she'll be continuing to learn about cause and effect.

Emotional and social development

Your baby is learning that being friendly is rewarding because of the way you respond to her with cuddling, love, and soothing sounds. Now that she understands this, she will smile even more, knowing that you will smile back. She will also welcome you with definite waves and wriggles when she knows you are coming to her.

Recognition

One of the most significant developments that your baby's sharpened memory brings is that she now has a very detailed memory of the people closest to her, so she can recognize them as individuals. This starts to influence the way she interacts with you, your partner, her siblings, and anyone else she has a lot of contact with. For example, now that she knows you, she may have very distinct responses to your voice, which are quite different to her responses to your partner's voice: seeing or hearing you may calm her down, while hearing her father's voice may make her excited, for instance.

Happy talk

Your baby's different little noises are beginning to be recognizable now.

She is becoming more skilled at expressing herself. For example, she may show her feelings of pleasure by making attempts to "coo" to you. She may even shriek with pleasure, and even giggle to express her delight. She will also be learning that loud screeching will bring you running to her side – another lesson in cause and effect!

Although your baby cannot repeat any words, she is listening to you and storing them all for the future, so the more you talk to your baby, the better for her.

Activities to develop skills

Now that your baby is responding to you and conversing with you more, you will have even more fun playing and interacting with her. She still needs all the cuddling and words of encouragement and reassurance, but you can expand your repertoire with more adventurous activities such as bouncing games and sing-alongs. Try lying her on her stomach from time to time. Roll a ball toward her and let her stretch toward it. As she plays, she is strengthening her neck, arm, and leg muscles.

Touching and kicking

★ Let your baby touch toys or objects of different textures, temperatures, and materials: fur, silk, velvet, water, warm skin. Let her lie on a play mat that has materials of different textures sewn carefully into it or Velcroed to it.

Singing games

★ Gently bounce your baby on your knee to the beat of your baby's favorite song,

★ Sing splashing songs in the bath, counting songs when you play with her fingers, lullabies when it's time to go to sleep – she'll love them all!

★ Try patting out the rhythm of the songs on her tummy or hands as you sing to her. This will give your baby even more enjoyment.

FLEECY COMFORT
This baby is clearly delighted at the comforting, soft feel of this warm, fleecy rug on his legs as his mother sits him in the middle of it.

3 to 4 months

This month, your baby's increasing knowledge and understanding is transferred into action. He is really growing in strength and ability, with each new experience being stored in his memory. You will also notice that he has become far more responsive to the people around him, smiling, gurgling, and laughing to express himself and communicate with his favorite person – you.

Physical development

During this month your baby will take a real leap forward in the way he can control his movements. When he lies on his stomach, he will probably now easily lift his head and upper body off the ground, supporting himself quite well with his arms and hands, and turning his head to you or anything that interests him. He will be able to hold his head steady for a short while.

Movement

His developing neck control marks the beginning of a whole new adventure for your baby. His increased strength, confidence, and ability to maneuver himself up on to his hands means that sometime over the next three months, much to his surprise – and yours – he will suddenly find himself rolling over. Do not leave him unattended on a bed or changing mat, for example, since he might choose this moment to roll over for the first time, and fall off.

This is an important milestone, as he is gaining a sense of control over his whole body, paving the way for learning to crawl in later months.

Learning skills

Your baby's brain is growing at a tremendous rate, and this is reflected in his increased curiosity. He will now love being supported in a sitting position in a bouncer seat or an infant rocker, and may complain if he is left for too long lying on his back. He is eager to take in everything around him – especially new faces, toys, and sounds.

Sound and vision

Your baby will be making even more effort to make his own sounds in response to you or your partner when you talk to him.

His eyesight will have greatly improved since those first hazy newborn days, and he can now use both eyes together to focus on something, whether it's close up or right on the other side of the room.

Increasing hand control

Your baby's hand control will be becoming far more refined, and by now he may be able to grab hold of a rattle or toy if you give it to him, although he will not be able to let go of it as yet.

★ He will be fascinated by what his hands can do. They, along with his mouth, are his tools for the exploration of his world. He will use his hands for searching out and exploring parts of his own face, such as his nose and his mouth, clutching at new and interesting objects. He will also use one hand simply to play with the other.

★ He will still enjoy swiping at toys within reach and will occasionally manage to grab hold of one. However, he won't quite know what to do with the toy – except, of course, to put it in his mouth to explore it with his tongue and mouth.

★ He will be intrigued by the sensation of holding different textured objects, such as a soft, squishy toy and a cool, smooth, plastic one.

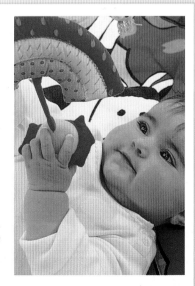

FIRM GRASP
This baby successfully grabs hold of one of the hanging soft toys on her cradle gym and tries resolutely to pull it toward her.

This means that he is more able to judge the distance between himself and the things he is looking at, so his hand–eye coordination will be much better now.

This clarity of vision also means he can clearly focus even on something as small as a button, and follow a moving object, if held a few inches away from him. When the object disappears, you may notice him continuing to stare at the space where he last saw it.

Amazing memory

Your baby's memory is now really being put to use, and you will probably notice that he is learning

quite quickly. For instance, the first time he shook a rattle was purely accidental. But he will have stored information about how the rattle feels, its color, the way it sounded when his hand moved, and your reaction that he did something clever. After this, each time he holds a rattle, his behavior will become more purposeful.

Emotional and social development

Your baby will not only smile when you smile now, he may even laugh out loud in delight when you do something that he enjoys. He is

enjoying himself, and at the same time he's learning how to get you to laugh and respond warmly to him. In fact, he'll love to make you laugh – it's instant positive feedback. He will know that you're pleased with him and also that he's got your complete attention.

Getting a response

Your baby has now learned to expect a response when he does something – if he smiles he'll expect you to smile back, and if he wants your attention he may try to initiate a conversation himself by cooing or gurgling. This brings a whole new dimension of enjoyment to your

Toy box

Ball play

Your baby will be fascinated by objects that move – especially if he can control them. Try lying him on his tummy and rolling a brightly colored ball in front of him across his line of vision, about 2ft (60cm) away from his body.

At first he will intently watch the ball as it moves from one side to the other, but he will soon come to anticipate this action and try to reach out to grab it on all subsequent rolls.

Textured toys

Now that he is grabbing hold of things, it's worth giving your baby lots of different textures. Let him have a range of toys to explore: smooth plastic toys; toys that are squishy; beanie toys that change shape as you hold them; toys with bumpy surfaces. Make sure they are safe for a baby to play with before you buy them. His cradle gym and play mat may also become more fascinating now.

Glove and finger puppets

Glove puppets with fun faces can also be a great source of amusement – babies love looking at faces, as you've

probably noticed by now! Make your own out of an old sock – he'll love it just as much as one from the toy store. If you use buttons for eyes, do check that they are securely sewn on, as babies tend to put everything they can into their mouths, and if a button becomes detatched in his mouth it could make him choke.

interaction with him. He is learning to take the lead, which is important to his sense of self-confidence, and, as you follow his lead, you will learn even more about his emerging character and sense of fun.

Encourage him to feel confident by making sure you always give him a response and acknowledging all the efforts he makes to interact with you.

Feeling secure

At this stage, your baby will probably be naturally outgoing and not at all shy or self-conscious. He will charm everyone with his smile, and, although he'll prefer you to anyone else, he will love to "talk" to people – other babies, complete strangers, even his own reflection.

By now, you may have decided to start a routine of regular nap times, walks outside, feeding, baths, and bedtime. This helps him learn to anticipate the events of the day, and teaches him that his life has a pattern to it. It helps him feel emotionally secure and increases his confidence. Establishing a routine also helps him to trust that you are near, even if he cannot see you.

Having a structure to your day and getting out and about with your baby will increase your pleasure, too. You may find that it boosts your confidence and helps you feel in control of your new job as a parent.

Activities to develop skills

As your baby gains better physical control and is more aware of objects and his surroundings, the range of toys and games he will enjoy increases. Interaction with you is still his number-one pastime, and he will show even more enjoyment of singing, clapping, and bouncing games. They will now be familiar to him, which will boost both his enjoyment and confidence.

Repetitive actions

Now that he can recognize familiar objects, your baby may love to play repeatedly with a toy that can make a sound if moved in a particular way.

By singing simple, repetitive rhymes, he will soon recognize the tune (even if he doesn't yet understand the words) and anticipate the actions that go with it. Try the action song "Row, Row, Row Your Boat."

Playing with finger puppets

Your baby will be fascinated by the distinctive and friendly faces of finger puppets. Bring them to life by moving your fingers, perhaps integrating the movement with a song or story.

Lie your baby on your partner's chest and get his dad to hold up the finger puppets. When he reaches out, he'll be strengthening his muscles.

1 This baby is at first not sure what to make of these animal face finger puppets, although he is clearly intrigued by their friendly faces.

2 After a few minutes of play with the puppets, the baby, feeling more secure, reaches out to grab one to find out more about it. What does it feel like?

4 to 5 months

Your baby will now be making controlled movements and may be starting to use her limbs to maneuver herself by rolling from front to back. She's becoming more aware of new situations, can detect changes in atmosphere and mood, and is really expressing her feelings. Her new levels of coordination and understanding mean she will now begin to respond even more enthusiastically to new toys and games.

Physical development

Improved muscle control and understanding of what her body can do mean that your baby's movements are now quite deliberate – you will notice that she is much more effective in reaching and grabbing hold of what she wants or positioning herself on the floor to play, for example.

Keeping steady

She will now be able to hold her head steady when held upright, and will keep her head in line with her body without letting it lag behind when pulled from sitting – a major developmental milestone. Although she cannot support herself sitting up, she will definitely feel happiest propped up in a sitting position, so that she can keep an eye on what's going on around her and join in with everything. You may find she takes great delight in kicking the sides of her bath when she's in the water, or kicking out at any surface within reach of her toes.

Your baby will enjoy any activity that gives her a chance to push with her legs and feet – and doing this will help strengthen her muscles ready for crawling.

If you hold on to her hands she may try to bounce up and down, although she won't be able to hold a standing position for very long. Don't let go of her, since she does not yet have the muscle strength or physical coordination skills to take her own weight on her feet.

Learning skills

Your baby is increasing her non-verbal forms of communication, using her body to make her point: she will push you away if she wants to do something else; reach for something she wants to play with; or turn her head away to let you know she doesn't want something.

Talking to you

Your baby's ability to communicate with you through language is also becoming more sophisticated. She can deliberately change the tone or inflection of her sounds, showing you her discontent or frustration as well as her enjoyment and pleasure.

She is probably more vocal in letting you know what she wants by making particular babbling sounds, which mean "Pick me up" or "I want to play with that!"

Talking to her

Although she doesn't understand the meaning of your words yet, she will understand their tone. She will be very sensitive to the change of tone in your voice. A firm tone will stop

Coordination skills

Your baby's visual skills now mean that she is able to judge how far away a toy is and maneuver herself to reach out for it and grab it with one or both hands.

★ She will be able to hold a toy firmly in her grasp, with her fingers securely curled round it. If she holds a rattle, she may now know what to do with it (thanks to her improved memory!).

★ Her own body still holds great fascination for her, and she will love to grab hold of her foot and suck her toes when the mood takes her.

HAND–EYE COORDINATION
This baby is now able to judge how far away the ball is and reach out for it accurately.

her, but is also likely to make her cry. If overused, it will discourage her natural curiosity and learning later on. To help her grasp meaning, make lots of eye-to-eye contact, because it is through your facial expressions that she can assess situations and begin to understand what you are saying. By letting her watch you as you speak, you are continuing to lay important foundations that will later help her to form words through imitation. Reserve using "No!" for periods of danger.

Concentration skills

Your baby will really be able to concentrate now, and some toys, games, and activities will hold her interest for longer periods.

Not only will she hold a toy, she will examine it, manipulate it, and feel and taste it by putting it in her mouth. This is her most sensitive area, so it's a natural place for her to put things to find out more about them. Make sure that small objects are not within your baby's reach, since she could easily choke on them.

Emotional and social development

At this stage, your baby will really benefit from being part of everything that is going on. Encourage her, and acknowledge her when she makes her contributions – whether it's a gurgle or a hand lifted up with a toy in it to show you. Encourage everyone else to respond in this way, too. The more attention she gets from siblings, friends, and your partner, the better for her!

Activities to develop skills

Now that your baby is eager to interact with you rather than simply observe what you are doing, she will try to attract your attention to let you know when she wants to play. Keep her toys within easy reach for her, and respond when she guides you to what she wants by reaching for something. If she knows that you understand what she is communicating to you in this way, you will be giving her confidence a great boost.

Physical fun

Because your baby's upper body is so strong and her head control is complete, she will probably know how to roll over now from front to back. Try playing floor games with her that allow her show off her new skill to you and allow you to help her perfect it.

Action songs

There are plenty of songs you can sing to encourage your baby to use her limbs and improve her motor skills. Sing songs that have accompanying hand actions, such as "The Wheels on the Bus" and "Patty-cake, Patty-cake." Hold her hands or legs as you sing, so that she can join in the action.

Your baby's face is full of expression and she will show a wider range of emotions – frustration at not being able to grab something, distress if her favorite toy or bottle is taken away, gurgling with delight at seeing something that amuses her.

Security

Although she will probably be quite happy to be entertained by anyone, you are still her favorite person. She will raise her arms to be picked up when she sees you, and may start to become agitated if she sees you leaving the room. She'll feel most secure when she's in your arms and will react more readily to your voice.

Socializing

Although she will happily examine objects by herself and watch what is going on around her, she is getting more eager for social interaction, wanting to join in conversations that take place around her. She will also watch you intently while you show her how to play with a toy or play games together.

This interaction makes her feel part of the family, contributing to her emotional security and helping her develop her social skills. These extremely important skills fall into two categories: learning how others think and feel; and learning how to care about them.

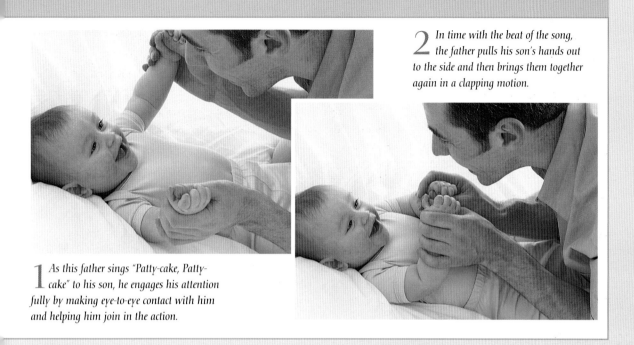

2 In time with the beat of the song, the father pulls his son's hands out to the side and then brings them together again in a clapping motion.

1 As this father sings "Patty-cake, Patty-cake" to his son, he engages his attention fully by making eye-to-eye contact with him and helping him join in the action.

Quick change

It can take only seconds for your happy, easy-going baby to dissolve into tears. A tickling game or splashing around in the bath can quickly turn from fun into tears, since there is a fine line between enjoyment and too much stimulation or excitement.

Try to anticipate these changes – perhaps they happen when she is tired, for example – and respond to them quickly. Remember that your baby still needs quiet time, and may even want to be alone for a while. By recognizing her need for a break, you can build trust and give her time to calm down and refocus.

Toy box

Surprise

Your baby will love games with an element of surprise. A jack-in-the-box, or a toy that makes a noise if you press it in a certain place, will be great fun now. Encourage her to interact and use her hand and visual skills by helping her to push down on toys to make them pop up.

Squeak?

Put a different squeaky toy into each of your baby's hands. Make sure they are pliable enough to make a noise with just one hand. Watch as she tries to figure out which hand the noise is coming from when she presses it.

Music and movement

Your baby will enjoy toys that she can manipulate easily. A baby tambourine will be great fun for her now, as will a clear plastic toy shaker with colorful beans inside that she can shake around. Both teach her about the power she has over things.

5 to 6 months

Six months is a developmental watershed for your baby as he grasps new concepts as well as physical skills. At around this time he will really be able to demonstrate his love for you and desire to be with you – he will want to touch your face, grab your hair, or hold out his arms to be picked up, for example.

Physical development

Your baby is growing in leaps and bounds, and each week brings new physical developments that increase the range of activities he can enjoy.

Mighty muscles
During this month or the next, your baby might learn to sit unsupported, although, for a while yet, most babies will still need some support when sitting. When he's lying down, the improved control he has over his limbs means he can now easily roll over onto his back from his front.

Keeping focused
Your baby's eyesight and his hand–eye coordination have improved so much that it is almost as good as yours. He can now deliberately reach for an object and bring it straight to his mouth. Faces are still his favourite thing to look at, and he is getting better at distinguishing facial expressions now. He can tell a happy face from a sad face.

Learning skills

Your baby is very eager to experiment with whatever he can lay his hands on, feeling toys for their different textures (and tastes!) and trying to figure out why it's more difficult to hold a large toy than a

Happy hands

Your baby's hands are still his key to exploring. Tasks that were beyond him just a couple of weeks back, such as rotating his wrist to inspect a toy, are now part of his physical repertoire. He can pick up small objects using his fist in a scooping action.

★ Your baby will start to pass an object from one hand to the other with his fist as he figures out what he wants to do with it. If he accidentally drops the object, he may reach down to try to retrieve it if it is within sight.

small one. He will increasingly be trying out cause and effect, too, noticing that when he shakes a certain toy it will make a noise while another one is silent, or swiping at some blocks to watch them fall across the floor.

Understanding
Your baby's greater comprehension of what is going on around him means that he will now concentrate on subjects for longer, whether it's looking at a toy in his hands or watching you.

He will focus intently on one thing at a time, mainly using just one sense – listening to music, watching you, or examining a picture in a book, or scooping up a building

block with his hands – before becoming distracted and moving on to a new activity.

Making conversation
Your baby is eager to communicate with you, and will try to make different sounds with his mouth.

He will practice using his tongue, poking it out and blowing raspberries with his lips to make different sounds. Listen to him carefully and you may notice that your baby is also becoming more adept at changing his tone of voice in the hope that you will turn and look at him as he realizes that people use different noises to communicate.

He is beginning to understand a little of what you say, too. He may turn his head toward you when he hears you use his name in conversation and will understand often-repeated words, such as "mommy" or "bedtime."

Emotional and social development

By now you will have a good idea of your baby's personality and his growing individual characteristics.

Social skills

Although he may still be quite happy to be held by strangers, he is now able to distinguish between people he knows and those he doesn't, and will show a definite preference for familiar faces – yours most of all!

He will get a lot of enjoyment from social situations, such as watching other children play, sitting in his highchair at family mealtimes, and being taken to the park. These events also help him to interact with other people, and feel comfortable in new situations when they occur.

Let him be a part of everything that is going on. Encourage him as he tries new things, and acknowledge him when he makes his own contributions – whether it's a gurgle or a hand lifted up with a toy in it to show you. Encourage everyone around him to respond to him in

this way, too. Siblings, friends, your partner – they will all be sources of endless fascination for your baby, and the more attention he gets from them, the better.

Getting emotional

Since your baby is now emotionally more mature, he will show a wider range of emotions in different situations. He can show you that he is excited by bouncing up and down, that he has seen something

that gives him joy by gurgling with pleasure, remaining quiet and watching warily when he is unsure of a situation, or crying when his needs are not met.

Personality changes

Although genes play a part in determining your baby's personality, he will already have developed many of his own characteristics, likes and dislikes. However, many of the traits you see in him now will not

Activities to develop skills

Your baby will probably need only minimum support when sitting up now, and is keen to explore and examine everything around him. He'll still love all the sing-alongs, bouncing games, and clapping games, and you will be able to be a little more physically playful with him now that he's stronger. He'll enjoy being tickled – try blowing raspberries on his tummy and see his delight!

Hide the teddy

To help your baby learn the concept of something being there when it cannot be seen, hide his teddy bear

under a blanket. Pull away the blanket and watch your baby's interested and surprised face as he watches something he thought was gone suddenly appear.

SURPRISE
This baby expresses surprise and indignation when her mother appears from behind the curtain. She was there all along!

necessarily stay with him for the rest of his life. For example, he may be impatient for solids at every meal or frustrated by not yet being able to move around freely and reach the things he wants, but this does not mean that he will grow into an impatient or frustrated child.

Remember that your baby has a long way to go before he can understand, reason, or use language to communicate effectively what he is thinking or wants.

Toy box

Mat exploration

His play mat will now be more useful. Athough he is not crawling yet, your baby will be able to move himself around a little by rolling or using his arms. A brightly colored activity mat with attached toys will keep him amused as he explores the different areas on it.

Cuddly toys

Your baby will love soft toys with faces now. Encourage him to be gentle with them – role-play by cuddling a favored teddy bear or puppet and saying "Aah" (to teach your baby about sociability, gentleness, and kindness). It won't be long before he will start "looking after" his toys, too.

Crib contentment

Your baby will appreciate a range of toys attached to the bars of his crib to play with when he wakes up or before he falls asleep. These are useful for amusing your baby for short periods, but are no replacement for interaction with you, your partner, and siblings.

Your baby may already have a favourite soft toy or blanket, which gives him a sense of security.

Plastic blocks

Your baby will be delighted at his own skill at pressing buttons on simple toys to make a face pop up or a noise to sound, as well as knocking down a tower of plastic blocks, or swiping at a roly-poly doll that rights itself after it has been pushed over.

Not only is he mastering his hand-eye coordination, but also learning about cause and effect.

1 This baby watches with enormous interest as her mother builds a tower with her colorful blocks. What will happen next?

2 The baby cannot restrain herself from knocking the tower over with her fists. She will not be satisfied until the tower is entirely demolished.

Index

allergies, 27, 36
Apgar score, 9

babbling, 24, 57
bedtime routines, 31–2
birth, 8–9
body language, 22
bonding, 8, 14, 16–17
books, 25, 47
bottle-feeding, 27–8
brain development, 21, 53
breast-feeding, 14, 26–7, 36
breathing, 8, 14–15

centile charts, 35
cesarean section, 8, 10
character traits, 20–1, 62–3
coordination skills, 57
co-sleeping, 32, 33
colostrum, 26
communication, 22–5
   see also language development
concentration, 58, 61
crawling reflex, 13
crib death, 33
crying, 11, 22–4, 43

depression, postpartum, 17
developmental checks, 12–13,
   34–5

eating, 29
emotional development, 42–3, 47,
   50–1, 54–5, 58–9, 62–3
expressing milk, 27
eye contact, 22, 24, 57–8
eyesight, 11, 41, 46–7, 50, 53–4,
   61

face, newborn baby, 10
fathers, bonding, 17
feeding, 26–9
fontanelles, 10

games, 42, 46, 51, 55, 58–9,
   62–3
gender differences, 20–1
genes, 20, 62
genitals, 11, 12
grasp reflex, 13, 34
growth charts, 35

hair, 11
hand control, 45, 49, 53, 57, 61
happiness, 43
head, newborn baby, 10
head control, 41, 45, 49, 53, 57
health checks, 12–13, 34–5
hearing, 11, 47

immune system, 27, 31
immunizations, 36

language development, 24–5, 42,
   47, 50–1, 57–8, 61–2
lanugo, 11

massage, 18–19
memory, 47, 49, 50, 54
milestones, 39
milk, 26–8
"milk spots," 11
Moro reflex, 13
movement, 41, 45, 53
muscle development, 41, 45, 49,
   53, 57, 61
music, 43, 51, 58–9

naps, 31, 32
newborn baby, 8–17

personality development, 20–1,
   62–3

physical development, 41, 45, 49,
   53, 57, 61
play, 7, 42, 46, 51, 55, 58–9, 62–3
postpartum blues, 17
postpartum depression, 17
premature babies, 14–15

recognition, 50
record keeping, 34
reflexes, 12–13, 27, 34

rolling over, 53, 58
rooting reflex, 27

security, 55, 58
senses, development of, 41
SIDS (Sudden Infant Death
   Syndrome), 33
singing games, 51, 58–9
sitting up, 57, 61
skin, newborn baby, 10–11
sleep, 30–3
smell, sense of, 11
smiling, 45
social development, 47, 50–1,
   54–5, 58–9, 62
solid food, 28–9, 36
speech see language development
sucking reflex, 13, 27

talking see language development
teething, 29
temperament, 21
toys, 43, 47, 50, 54, 58, 59, 63
twins, 15, 20

umbilical cord, 11

vernix, 10–11

walking reflex, 13
weaning, 28–9, 36
weight, 8–9, 35

Acknowledgments

The author would like to thank Pippa Duncan for all her help.

Credits
Jacket photo: Camille Tokerud/Getty Images
Jacket design: Nicola Powling
Indexer: Hilary Bird; **proof–reader:** Nikky Twyman
Models: Jo with Jade Salliger, Jason with Kasia Wall, Linda
with Mackenzie Quick, Simon with Oban Murrell, Rachana with
Arianna Shah, Penny with Anastasia Stephens, Thimmie with
Emily Pickering, Andrea with Joel Peters, Rachel with Zoe Nayani,
Rachel with baby Best, Isabelle with Carla Wicker-Jourdan, Alison
with Phoebe Lee; **hair and make–up:** Tracy Townsend

Consultants
Warren Hyer MRCP is Consultant Paediatrician at
Northwick Park and St. Mark's Hospitals, Harrow, and
Honorary Clinical Senior Lecturer, Imperial College of Science,
Technology and Medicine.
Penny Tassoni is an education consultant, author and trainer.
Penny lectures on a range of childhood studies courses and has
written five books, including *Planning, Play and the Early Years.*

Picture Credits
Picture researcher: Cheryl Dubyk-Yates
Picture librarian: Hayley Smith

The publisher would like to thank the following for their kind per-
mission to reproduce their photographs: (abbreviations key: t=top,
b=bottom, r=right, l=left, c=center)

Sally & Richard Greenhill Photo Library: Sally Greenhill
42c; **Robert Harding Picture Library**: Caroline Wood/Int'l
Stock 16bl; **The Image Bank**: Tosca Radigonda 27tr; **Mother &
Baby Picture Library**: Moose Azim 8bl; **Pictor International**:
12br, 35tl; **Science Photo Library**: John Greim 9tr; Ruth
Jenkinson 11tl; Publiphoto Diffusion 14bl; Peter Yates 29bl; Hattie
Young 10bl; **Corbis Stock Market**: Norbert Schafer 15br; Pete
Saloutos 34bl; **Superstock Ltd**: 25tr

All other images © Dorling Kindersley. For further information see:
www.dkimages.com